GOING FOR AN AUDITION?

The 100 monologues in this superb collection by playwright members of New York City's highly acclaimed New Dramatists provide you with fresh, outstanding dramatic monologues, some created specifically for this edition.

Each of these 100 monologues was tested in a simulated audition/workshop setting by professional actors with input from directors, casting directors, and dramaturgs. Length, overall effect, and the scene's ability to demonstrate an actor's range were prime considerations in the selection process.

A reporter in Vietnam . . . a mother recalling her daughter's birth . . . a divorced woman describing her love life . . . a husband arguing with his wife over having a baby . . . a former black child star recounting the old days . . . a 15th-century monk's terrifying passion: All these are great subjects and great scenes for actors who know that a successful audition depends on their talents, but starts with outstanding material.

100 MONOLOGUES
An Audition Sourcebook
from New Dramatists

100 Monologues
An Audition Sourcebook from New Dramatists

EDITED BY
Laura Harrington

A MENTOR BOOK

MENTOR
Published by the Penguin Group
Penguin Books USA Inc., 375 Hudson Street,
New York, New York 10014, U.S.A.
Penguin Books Ltd, 27 Wrights Lane,
London W8 5TZ, England
Penguin Books Australia Ltd, Ringwood,
Victoria, Australia
Penguin Books Canada Ltd, 10 Alcorn Avenue,
Toronto, Ontario, Canada M4V 3B2
Penguin Books (N.Z.) Ltd, 182–190 Wairau Road,
Auckland 10, New Zealand

Penguin Books Ltd, Registered Offices:
Harmondsworth, Middlesex, England

Published by Mentor, an imprint of Dutton Signet,
a division of Penguin Books USA Inc.

For copyrights and permissions, see pages 258–261, which constitute an
extension of the copyright page.

First Printing, May, 1989
10   9   8   7   6   5

REGISTERED TRADEMARK—MARCA REGISTRADA

Library of Congress Catalog Card Number: 88-63801

Printed in the United States of America

Contents

MONOLOGUES FOR WOMEN

CONTENTS

CONTENTS

MONOLOGUES FOR MEN

CONTENTS

CONTENTS

CONTENTS

APPENDICES

Acknowledgments

The following people were of enormous help in bringing this book to press:

Thanks to David Hill for coming up with the idea; to Susan Gregg, Stan Chervin, and Lynn Holst for helping to shape the idea; to Eileen Fallon for selling the idea; and to the New Dramatists staff, in particular, Thomas G. Dunn, Executive Director, David Milligan, Program Director, and Maren Swenson, Associate Program Director. Very special thanks to Mary Elizabeth Carlin, who served as my editorial assistant, and to Robert Lord and Jeff Fligelman, who were helpful in the early stages of putting this book together.

Special thanks to the actors, directors, casting directors, and dramaturgs who helped us workshop the monologues at New Dramatists:

Actors: John Baray   Felicity LaFortune
         Lisa Barnes   Hazel Medina
         Graham Brown   Michael Morin
         Mary Louise Burke   Katherine Neuman
         William Carpenter   Susan Pellegrino
         Steve Coates   Leon Russom
         Paul Collins   Socorro Santiago
         William Hao   Timothy Woodward
         Helen Harrelson

New Dramatists Board of Directors
October 1988

ACKNOWLEDGMENTS

Directors: Casey Childs
              Robert Hall
              Gideon Schein

Casting Director/Dramaturgs: Douglas Abel
                                      Jay Binder
                                      Judy Dennis
                                      Michael Fender
                                      Daniel Swee

The royalties from this book are being donated to the Stanley Young loan fund at New Dramatists.

Foreword

People who have heard me speak know that there is a sign over my desk which reads, "Nobody asked you to be a playwright." I put it there almost forty years ago to stop my bitching.

Although the message is still lamentably true—talented playwrights are wooed by television and movie producers, but rarely hear a "How are you doing?" from theatre producers—there was a time, soon after we all came back from World War II, when people were asking us to be playwrights.

The honorable and venerable Theatre Guild had a group of young playwrights meeting under the guidance of John Gassner and Theresa Helburn. Theatre Incorporated, a new producing firm, gathered some of us with Theodore Apstein keeping order. The American Theatre Wing, which had been so active during the war with projects such as The Stage Door Canteen, set up a whole "academy" where they sponsored refresher courses for returning veterans.

Mary Hunter, who was the academic head of this Professional Training Program, approached me to teach the playwriting courses. Barely a playwright myself (I had had one Off-Broadway production), I started the courses and taught myself and a fair number of other young playwrights. I can still see myself rushing into class full of enthusiasm about what I had just found out that morning about writing plays.

Distinguished guests such as Howard Lindsay, Elia Kazan, Arthur Miller, and Moss Hart came to share their experiences and wisdom with us. And once a week the students' plays were read aloud by a group of neophyte actors including Eileen Heckart, Jean Stapleton, and Harry Belafonte. The Wing also received free tickets to the theatre.

At the same time a young playwright, Michaela O'Harra, with one Broadway production to her credit, felt the theatre industry itself should offer some "growing ground for *all* qualified new dramatists." Since Howard Lindsay had been extraordinarily supportive of my program at The Theatre Wing, I suggested to Michaela that she solicit his advice and help. Her passion for the idea was contagious, and she persuaded Howard to become the godfather of her venture.

And so with the support of Howard Lindsay and Russell Crouse, The Dramatists Guild, The Playwrights Company, Richard Rodgers and Oscar Hammerstein and John Golden, the New Dramatists was started in 1949.

For some years the dedicated Michaela ran the organization almost single-handedly, with occasional help from other New Dramatists like Eva Wolas. Our office was the small cloakroom in the Hudson Theatre (owned by Lindsay and Crouse), and we met in a large, dimly lit conference room five flights up at the top of the theatre. There, week after week, we neophytes gathered to listen to the likes of Lindsay, Robert Sherwood, Maxwell Anderson, Elia Kazan, S. N. Behrman, Moss Hart, and others. Those early New Dramatists eager for every word included Bill Inge, Paddy Chayefsky, Bill Gibson, Horton Foote, Joe Kramm, Ronald Alexander, and Sumner Locke Elliot among others, who in due time would themselves return to talk to new generations of New Dramatists including James Goldman, Michael Stewart, Max Wilk, Joe Masteroff, Arnold Schulman, Jack Gelber, Lanford Wilson, who would in due time . . .

When someone had a play ready, he or she would read it to us and bravely listen to the comments. Thanks to the producers, we went to the theatre free. We felt appreciated.

Over the years we grew out of the cloakroom to offices in City Center with Michaela still firmly at the helm, but aided now by such administrators as the late George Hamlin and the casting and production wizard, Robert Colson.

Now we have our own building, an old church, which contains two theatres and is located on the same block as the old church housing the Actors Studio. (It's a nice picture, the playwrights and the actors developing side by side.) There is a large staff headed by the indefatigable and resourceful Tom Dunn. The nature of the group has shifted over the years. The playwrights are more sophisticated, many of them having had productions in regional, Broadway, Off- and Off-Off Broadway theatres.

The New Dramatists is still a place for talented playwrights to develop, to grow, to work in a theatre with fine actors and directors with no production pressures. In the years since New Dramatists was founded, many valuable nurturing grounds have sprung up around the country. All are doing notable work. The New Dramatists, however, is unique. Upon admittance, the writer becomes a member for five years—five years to hear his plays read, see them performed, listen, learn from the efforts of others, see theatre, enjoy the support and companionship of other playwrights and the services of a trained staff of people who are there to help the playwright grow and develop. There is no charge for all this. The only requirements are talent and a willingness to pursue a goal.

We point with pride to the work of the member playwrights who over the years have shared their talents and wisdom and caring and who have emerged—if not Pulitzer Prize winners, as four of our members have—at least to a better understanding of their art and craft.

—Robert Anderson
Original New Dramatists Member
Current Member, Board of Directors

Introduction

We hope that *100 Monologues* will be Volume One in a series. The book was created to provide new material for actors who are auditioning. Some of the monologues in this collection were written specifically for this book, others are excerpts from unpublished plays, and still others come from published plays. But most of the monologues included here have not been seen or heard before.

To ensure that these pieces will work in an audition, we spent time with actors, directors, casting directors, and dramaturgs, "workshopping" the material. The workshop format gave us the opportunity to see the monologues on their feet in simulated audition situations. Playwrights revised, rewrote, and tightened their monologues. The result is a book full of new material that has nonetheless been tested.

When we first wrote to the New Dramatists member playwrights asking them to submit monologues for the book, we made a special point of asking for monologues for ethnic as well as white actors, for sixty-year-olds as well as sixteen-year-olds. We wanted to create a collection of monologues that would appeal to a wide spectrum of talented actors. However, rest assured that the majority of material here is appropriate for the average age of an actor auditioning today—25–35. If you are an actor looking for a monologue that helps you demonstrate your range, you should find it here.

If you happen to become intrigued by a writer's work and would like to read more, we've provided the publishers' names or the words: "Available at New Dramatists." Any of the plays so designated can be found and read in the National New Play Library of New Dramatists, 424 West 44th Street, New York, NY 10036. At the back of the book we've also included a list of the plays and playwrights, as well as a note on whom to write for further information about the plays.

—Laura Harrington
Editor
New Dramatists Member Writer

100 MONOLOGUES
An Audition Sourcebook
from New Dramatists

Monologues
for
Women

SOLITAIRE/DOUBLE SOLITAIRE
by Robert Anderson

Charley and Barbara, a middle-aged couple, are experiencing a marriage crisis. Each mate discusses his or her marital troubles with a friend or relative. In this monologue, Sylvia, "an extremely stylish woman around forty," talks to Barbara about the failure of her marriage and the various men in her life now.

SYLVIA: I wouldn't get married again for a million dollars. I was a boring wife. I came to know exactly what I was going to say on every occasion and said it . . . Oh, I read all the books on how to be a thousand different women for your husband . . . On one occasion I even suggested an innovation or two in our sex life which had the unfortunate effect of blocking him completely for two weeks. So I finally persuaded him to divorce me (sans alimony, of course. I have my own shop and I wasn't going to fleece him because I was a frumpy bore). I lost ten pounds and immediately became more attractive and interesting—at least to myself. "Don't you get lonely?" they ask me. Who has time to be lonely? "Who do you see?" My God, I see their husbands. Not my friends' husbands, of course. I use some discretion. And it's not all sex, or even mostly . . . I find that every man has enough interesting happen to him in a week to fill one evening's conversation.

Mondays, I see this movie bug. He has to sit near the screen, and his wife has to sit far back. For years they compromised and sat in the middle and spoiled it for both of them. Also, she is an easy weeper and cries at almost everything, which annoys him and makes him feel insensitive. And he laughs easily, which makes her feel she has no sense of humor . . . So . . . Tuesdays I see this man who loves games, particularly *Scrabble*. His wife thinks games are frivolous, and besides, she can't spell . . . Wednesday is matinee day, and there's this sweet older man. He doesn't like to sit up late, so we have an early dinner after the matinee and I go home and get to bed early. A-lone. He's just had a heart attack, so that's why I'm free today . . . Thursdays I have lunch with this nice homosexual boy. That takes care of my mothering instincts . . . Thursday nights there's this man who likes to come and just sit in my neat, pretty, attractive apartment. His sexual relations with his wife are marvelous, but she's a slob about her house. So he just comes and sits in my apartment and we talk. Each shaking his head . . . Friday and Saturday nights are heavy date nights . . . Sundays I have *The New York Times*, and I do my other reading to keep up with the various interests of my dates—*Scientific American, Art News, Cahiers du Cinema, Fortune, Sports Illustrated* . . .

Now and then, of course, one of them asks me to marry him. A kind of conditioned reflex learned at Mother's knee—to make an honest woman of me. I find they usually ask at just about the time they're getting tired of making an effort. They're ready to take me for better or worse or for granted . . . I much prefer to be a visitor in a person's life. I get treated with much more consideration. Of course, it gets lonely on Mother's Day and Christmas and other tribal times when families rush off to graduations and weddings, bar mitzvahs, and circumcisions . . . But what the hell. I have a little warm dog who sleeps in my bed—when no one else is there, naturally. Some men are really thrown by having a dog stand there watching them.

(SYLVIA *Laughs*.)

They say I'll be lonely when I'm old. Well, I can always take a few pills or cut my throat . . . I mean, life was meant to be lived, not just endured.

[Published by Dramatists Play Service]

CAKES WITH THE WINE
by Edward M. Cohen

Sonny and his family have come to visit his sister, Blossom, after a long estrangement. There is a great deal of tension in the room which Blossom tries to bury with this supposedly funny tale from their childhood. She addresses it to Sonny's frightened son, Michael, in an effort to calm him.

BLOSSOM: Did your father ever tell you, Michael, about the time I went to audition for the radio? How scared I was? Did you, Sonny?

(SONNY *refuses to answer.* BLOSSOM *turns back to* MICHAEL *and tries again.*)

Radio was the big thing then and I wanted to be a singer. So I make an appointment to audition, and when the time comes, what do you know, I decide to go. I told Sonny I was going to the movies because he would have had a fit. I mean, he had a fit anyway because I never—I don't think I'd ever—been out of the house alone at night. I was maybe fifteen years old and he was my big brother who I adored and I always listened to everything he said. Didn't I, Sonny?

(*No answer from* SONNY.)

I had a silk print dress and I bought a special hat for the occasion. It was one of those pillboxes they wore with a feather that flapped in the back. Remember, Sonny?

(*No answer. Giggling,* BLOSSOM *demonstrates how the feather flapped.*)

I was nearly out of my mind with terror and I'm walking down Delancey Street—listen to this, Michael. It was pitch black, maybe nine o'clock, on the way to the subway, and I hear these footsteps behind me. Can you imagine? I keep turning my head and I hear this fellow sliding into doorways, but I'll be damned, I never spotted him. So I cross the street and, pitter-pat, pitter-pat, he's following after. Oh Jesus, I thought, I should have listened to Sonny and I end up running home like a maniac, to hell with the audition and, believe me, I tried to scream, but I couldn't find my voice because I still heard the footsteps in my ear, louder and louder. And I end up, banging on the door, screaming for Sonny and he takes me in his arms and I tell him the whole story.

(*Pause.* BLOSSOM *turns to* SONNY.)

It was my hat, wasn't it, Sonny? It was the feather flapping that I heard. Right? That's all there was to be afraid of.

(*Pause.*)

I took that hat off . . . and I wrapped it in tissue . . . and I never wore it again.

[Available at New Dramatists]

THE COMPLAINT DEPARTMENT CLOSES AT FIVE
by Edward M. Cohen

When they were young, Estelle and Hershey both worked for Ben Segal Appliance. Estelle quit when they were married, expecting Hershey to become store manager. But things did not turn out that way. For the first time in all these years, the powerful Ben Segal calls, announcing that he is coming over for an important talk. On the phone, Estelle flirts with him and reminds him of who she was, how she worked for him years ago when she was young and pretty. Now they await Ben Segal's arrival, convinced that he is coming to fire Hershey. Hershey gets so worried, he runs off to the bathroom to throw up. Estelle listens for the downstairs buzzer in terror.

ESTELLE (*Talking to* HERSHEY): I don't like it, Hershey. I don't like it one bit. A boss doesn't come unless it's bad. If you're losing your job after so many years, that would be the last straw!

(HERSHEY *leaves the room.*)

To have you turn into an out-of-work bum like my

father, who never earned a dime in his life while my mother coughed herself sick behind a candy-store counter! That's too much to ask of a person, Hershey!

My sister marries a dumb barber who turns into the head chair at the Waldorf Astoria and knows famous people by first name, and my husband, who was such a fancy dresser that everybody said he couldn't miss, turns into a silent Sam like my father, who was so afraid of his own shadow he couldn't take care of a candy store without losing half the stock!

Don't you forget how I fell in love the minute I met you because where my father was quiet, Hershey was loud. Where my father was glum, Hershey was happy. Where my father was frightened, Hershey was brave! The sun rose and set on your shoulders, Hershey, and day by day I see you turning into Papa, and if you lose your job and there comes a day when I look in the mirror and I don't see me, I see my mother? If that happens and it means my whole life has gone up in smoke, what will you say to me then?

(*Door buzzer rings.*)

My god! Hershey! He's downstairs!

(*Buzzer rings again.*)

Hershey! Please! What should I do?

(*It rings again.* ESTELLE *is paralyzed.*)

I never should have made such a fuss about my red hair, he's going to expect some beauty queen. He's got a picture in his mind of this nineteen-year-old, giggling, blushing, afraid to say a word, stapling cellophane bags in his warehouse.

(*Automatically* ESTELLE *goes through factory gestures with her hands.*)

Accessory Pre-Pack Thirty A. Phonograph needle.

Dust cloth, arm brush. I was terrific at my job because I knew every pre-pack by heart. He told me so himself. And my hands could work though my mind was a hundred miles away, dreaming about my wedding . . . I never should have told him it's still red . . It's not even gray, god knows. Just faded. No color, I suppose.

[Available at New Dramatists]

DON'T BREATHE ON THE JOB
by Allen Davis, III

The woman speaking in this monologue is Puerto Rican and needs a job badly. Her story, as told in the monologue, is self-contained.

WOMAN: This is what happened. I am recommended for a secretary job at this big corporation. The man who hires greets me and gives me coffee. He is about to order a pizza which he offers me—no, first he asks, "Do you prefer rice or beans?" and I joke with him that I do not need rice or beans three times a day, but he does not laugh. So he sends out for pizza, extra pepperoni in my honor.

I do not feel comfortable, but this is a good-paying job and I need it. He tells me they have no Spanish employees in the front office, and the big, liberal boss thinks this is a terrible oversight. I tell him, yes it is, and he says, "I thought Puerto Ricans were Puerto Ricans," and I say, oh no, Puerto Ricans are definitely Hispanic. So he thinks for a second and says, "Maybe that's even better. I mean, you're almost an American, right?" He says the big, liberal boss insists on a real Spanish secretary, so I simply say I am real and Spanish, and he replies, "You may be too real. We want someone Spanish, but not too Spanish."

I don't understand, but I need this job badly. My husband's pay is not enough, so I say I will be as Spanish as he wants and that I type ninety words a minute, take shorthand, and am experienced on the Wang. I remark I know I am a little darker than some Hispanics, and he jumps in: "We have no discrimination because of race, religion, or color. We only have discrimination because of oversights. In fact, we prefer the person we hire not to be too light because then she would look and sound like an American, and that wouldn't be fair to the Spanish." I assure him I can improve on my accent, and he says, "Oh no, your accent is perfect. Very believable."

I do not understand any of this. They want a Latino, but they don't want a Latino, but they don't want an American either. He tells me, "Of course, I will need to see your citizenship papers." I remind him I am Puerto Rican. My father was drafted into the Marines. He becomes agitated because he is not sure the big, liberal boss will be convinced a Puerto Rican is a real Spanish-type person without a piece of paper telling him so. I promise him a piece of paper showing that my parents were born in Santurce, Puerto Rico. He asks if it is near San Juan, and I reply it is on the same island. Now he says, "I must have your birth certificate and a list of all the places you and your parents lived. I must make double sure of this." I am getting as nervous as this man, but I say fine, fine, I will get a list together. Does this mean I have the job? He says there should be no problem, but first he must explain to me, "In the front office we don't allow low-cut

dresses, stiletto heels, and no long red fingernails."
And there I sit in my only Laura Ashley, but he does
not see me, so I begin to get angry. He warns me
some more: "You must be extra careful not to agitate
the men in the office—no long eyelashes, no beauty
marks on the bosom." My blood is enraged. I tell him
I am here to work, only to work, to do a good job.
That is all. "Good," he said, "just watch how you
breathe on the job—no heaving chests . . ."

Right then the pizza arrives, and before I can think,
I lift it off the tray and am about to heave it in his face
when I see the sticky cheese and pepperoni dripping
on his word processor keys. He is frightened, he is
angry, he cringes, he cries, "Oh my god—a spitfire." I
do not get the job.

[Available at New Dramatists]

SALLY'S GONE, SHE LEFT HER NAME
by Russell Davis

In this monologue Sally is speaking to her mother, who in the last year has become more and more withdrawn. Her mother has become like a specter—she doesn't want anything, and has suppressed all urges. This monologue begins with Sally trying to tell her mother it's okay to want, to be restless. But by the end of the monologue Sally is fully caught up in speaking of her own restless urge to get out, to be free and travel.

SALLY: Mom, it's not so bad to be restless. It's good. I get restless too. Mom, I do. 'Cause I don't want to be with Bruce or argue with Dad. I don't want to be home. I want something more. I want what Grandpa had. I want how he painted. Like his girl—I want to be the girl Grandpa painted. I don't want to be like us. More than anything, I know I want to be in that picture. Something like that picture. I want to go wear that wide headband she's got around her head. And that T-shirt. I want that extra-large T-shirt that's so light you can see through it. I want to go running like that in the middle of the night, more than anything I know, far away from anybody, any town, any teachers, family. Just run up and down, visit the ocean, and the mountains, everything. Yeah. Because I think if I could do that, be some kind of little-girl spirit all over again, if I could do that and not miss all the stuff, everything in my life, the people, the things to do, then I would be happy. I could be happy in a way that I could walk around for sixty years or so until I died, wearing nothing but this white T-shirt and a headband. Except on the headband I've embroidered: "Sally's gone." That's right. Sally's gone. And she's left her name, so don't try calling after her. She left her name.

In this second monologue, Sally is speaking to her brother Christopher. Their mother has left the house and Sally feels very much at fault. She had intended something much better than this. This monologue, however, is not a complaint, or a whine, but a recognition of something, a realization. In the midst of all that has happened, the bad thing she has caused, she has come to understand something. She feels a sense of gratitude.

SALLY: I really feel the things we speak to ourselves in our heads, the hopes, you know, they don't sound as good when you say them out loud. They don't sound like you just thought them. I don't know, because there's some kind of background music, in your head, and it isn't there even if you say exactly the same words.

For example, if I say in my head, I love you, Christopher, there's a background music. I don't mean there's music, but something, and I can get goosebumps on my arms from thinking about you. I love you, Christopher. Or if I said, I'm sorry. I'm sorry I made what happened to Mom. I never meant what happened to Mom. I don't know how I got so angry to make what happened.

(*Pause.*)

If I said that, immediately I would feel phony or something's awkward. And we'd have to argue right away to get back to normal. And I don't understand how come. How come you have to keep it in your head. How come the older you get, the more and more stuff you have to keep in your head. Any kind of hopes you ever had about living, all of it inside your head, until you can't hold it up anymore, and you're ashamed, and you fall over, get old, and die.

(*Pause.*)

I love you, Christopher

(*Pause.*)

I love you, too, Mom.

(*Pause.*)

I love you, Mom, from as far away as you have to get from me.

[Published by Theatre Communications Group "Plays in Process"]

DEAR
by R. Drexler

DEAR takes place in the Fifties and is about Jessie Culp, a Perry Como fan in her middle years. She is separated from her husband, has a gentleman friend, and a daughter she'd like to groom for stardom. Her real life is her fantasy life, the time she spends with Perry: she watches him religiously every Saturday night; he "visits" her and they discuss his career, her life, etc. In a contest, Jessie Culp wins a Charley Como puppet. She believes him to be her child and Perry Como the father. When Perry ignores her "son," she "gets rid" of C.C. and writes Perry a letter of condolence.

JESSIE: Beloved, I have taken care of that wonderful gift you sent me during the cruise. The gift known as C.C., who lived and breathed through me after you. He was all I had. Though you were what I wanted. Honey, I was willing to be a slave to you. I even rubbed lotion into my hands every time I did the dishes, and took regular diathermy in the clinic. I spent part of my money on a static-dust remover for your records. I taught Charley your songs and he inherited your talent. But life was never right and so I want to tell you that C.C. died on Thursday Eventide: May God rest his loving soul. He will never get involved with lonely and sick women the way you do, and he has reached heaven as quick as was possible. There are many wonderful thoughts in "Let's Go To Church Next Sunday Morning." Thank you, darling, for telling me you understood. I want you to believe in me in all ways and not to listen to those who would have you believe that I want to have sex with you. I have no objection to it, but would be tortured with remorse if it should interrupt your desperate period of mourning. Can't you feel that we are very close again? You were such a nice chap to sing "Where Will You Be When the Moon Shines?" Of course, with my devastating sense of humor I thought I'd thrown so much mud at you in my last few letters that you were disgusted and wanted to set a good example. You know where I'll be? I'll be wearing a black dress and black shoes, black nylons, black slip, black brassiere, and black undies. Seriously, when you sang "Let's Go Through Life Side by Side" you were thinking, I'm sure, of praying as the greatest means of attaining your wish. By the way, I'm not sure if I'm divorced or not, since I still have Mr. Culp's name. Notice the C and what it means. Notice the P and what it means. Parts of his name are known for what they mean everywhere—and now I'm stuck with it. By the way, I'll copy the St. Anthony prayer and enclose it. Any prayer would do, I presume, but this one is very beautiful and complete. Aren't you sorry you never took the dear departed out to dinner and a good show? I saved his bow tie for you in case you were sorry and wanted to have something of him. God bless you and keep you and until next week when we meet again through the written word, dream beautiful dreams, sweetheart. I love you, precious heart, with all my heart, eternally.

(JESSIE *picks up her pen and leans back over the paper. She speaks as slowly as she writes.*)

Yours, Jess (Jes' a wearyin' for you).

[Available at New Dramatists]

CHOCOLATE CAKE
by Mary Gallagher

CHOCOLATE CAKE is an encounter between two women, which may change the life of one of them. Annmarie is an uncertain young woman who is trying to fill her empty life with compulsive eating. She is sought out by an older woman, Delia, who has been filling her life in that same way for many years, has embraced it as her fate, and sees no way out. "You're a member of my club," she tells Annmarie. Plunged into the sorry world of Delia's bleak present, Annmarie sees her own probable future if she doesn't change her life, and it scares her.

ANNMARIE: Well . . . I—I put on a lot of weight . . . after I married Robbie. But I never can seem to stay on a diet more than a day or two. I mean, there's Robbie all the time . . . and when I have to cook pork chops and hash browns and biscuits and applesauce for him, it seems so dumb to just sit there watching him eat—hearing him chew—while I'm playing with carrot sticks . . . especially when he keeps telling me how tasty everything is and what a great little cook I am. Most of the time, he never says a word about my cooking. Just when I'm on a diet. At least it seems like that . . . So then, even if I make it through dinner and TV, which is real hard, with Robbie drinking beer and eating snacks . . when we get in bed, every time, here comes Robbie in his pj's with a great big root beer float. He has this mug he got in high school football that says "SPUDS." That was his nickname in high school, because he loved potatoes. I even call him Spuds sometimes still . . . for fun, you know. Anyway, he always uses that great big mug when he makes a root beer float. So there I am in bed, in my see-through nightie, with my hair fluffed up and all . . . and he gets in right beside me and starts making noises. Like "mmmmm."

So I say, "Robbie, you're just mean." And Robbie says, "Come on, Annie, you know you hate this diet stuff. And you don't need it. You look good, you look like a woman. You're always beautiful to me." I say, "Well, you sure don't act like it." Then he says, "Come on, Annie." And he eats his root beer float. And then he goes to sleep.

And then . . . I lie there—as long as I can stand it—and then I get up and put my bathrobe on—the old one with the holes. And I go in the kitchen, and I make myself a great big root beer float. It's twice as big as Robbie's. I make it in the orange juice pitcher. And I eat the whole thing standing up right there at the counter. And then I work my way back through the day. I eat whatever Robbie left at dinner, and whatever I didn't have for lunch because it was too fattening, and whatever I skipped at breakfast . . . and then I work my way through the refrigerator and the cupboards, I eat every single thing I can get my hands on that I shouldn't eat, peanut butter and banana sandwiches! And taco chips and sour cream dip! And fried potato sticks! And pop tarts! And Frosted Flakes right out of the box! And Oreos that I dip in Cool Whip! And sticky buns! And Girl Scout cookies that are still half frozen from the freezer! And then I realize that I'm eating things that I don't even like! Things that taste terrible! Stale Cheese Doodles, and hard marshmallows, and moldy coffee cake! And baking chocolate! And old nasty Easter candy that's all stuck together! And those little flower decorations that you put on birthday cakes! I mean, I don't care! I just eat everything! Everything! Everything that's bad.

[Published by Dramatists Play Service]

LIVING AT HOME
by Anthony Giardina

Mary Langtree is a Radcliffe sophomore and a "really all right" girl, according to her date, John. After a drink or two at the kitchen table, John persuades Mary to reveal what happened on the night of her senior prom. Mary, her boyfriend, and three other couples drove to a lake in New Hampshire to go swimming.

MARY: I guess I must have gotten pretty far out, because I couldn't hear anything anymore. Only Gordon's voice calling me from somewhere. Then a splash and a steady rippling of water, and then Gordon's face was beside me in the water, and I had to laugh, he suddenly looked so stupid, just this maze of yellow hair and two eyes and a nose and a mouth full of teeth, all of it wet, and there was all of a sudden no more of a person there than I might have felt in a fish or a seal that had swum up beside me. Just some happy animal that I had nothing whatsoever to do with.

(*Beat.*)

And the next thing was—out in the middle of this lake was a small island. I'd never really noticed it when we'd been to the lake before, but suddenly here it was, right in front of us—and I remember thinking. Now what is this doing here? Because it was obvious that the happy animal and I would have to somehow deal with its being there. We couldn't swim around it.

(*Beat.*)

So we stood up. That is, *he* stood up. I sat there on the edge of the sand, letting the water run up my suit and down it because I *loved* the way it felt. And here we were on this tiny little Eden, and I knew exactly what the happy animal was thinking, if he was thinking anything at all—it was like God or somebody had put this island here for us tonight—and then of course I was being kissed all over, but not really *there* at all, somewhere else, and my beautiful new black bathing suit was being taken off me and thrown aside. My one clear action, the one thing I, my real self, remembers doing, was breaking apart to retrieve the suit. But by that time it was too late. It had gotten washed away.

(*Beat.*)

So I sat there, waiting for it to come back. All of a sudden I was obsessed by what I had been when I bought it. Different. I mean, I suddenly felt so different from the girl who had gone into Filene's on the damn trolley to buy herself a bathing suit. I liked *her* so much, and I hated myself just then.

(*Beat.*)

The last thing I remember was Gordon—he was Gordon now, he'd regained something of a personality, asking me what the matter was. I wanted to swim. I said that. Maybe it was just in my head, but I remember saying that—I just wanted to swim.

[Published by Dramatists Play Service]

SCENES FROM LA VIE DE BOHEME
by Anthony Giardina

Joria is punk and is presently chopping off all her hair—"And this my hair, I'm trying to make it real slick, to say, kind of, You think you know me?" In response to her boyfriend John's request to remove a set of false male genitalia she had donned, Joria asks him if he's frightened by it. She explains that it's okay for him to be attracted to other men because she's up for anything.

JORIA: It's okay by me. You don't have to put up no false fronts for me. Be outrageous, Johnny. Some night, come to bed, don't have no penis. Who gives a shit? Like David Bowie in *The Man Who Fell to Earth*, like you take off your humanness you're just this pure gland. I mean, we could throb. Human beings homosapiens guy gets into bed humpa humpa d'jou have an orgasm honey yeah I had a good one honey, d'jou? Mine was okay, honey, g'night.
(JORIA *mimics snoring.*)
Oh man, I see like these other possibilities I see like

these guys, floating around watching us they see us, y'know, and they wonder, okay, when are they gonna get it on? And every once in a while they see us gettin' into bed and up pops this teeny tiny thing and the one who doesn't have a thing she spreads her legs and humpa humpa—they think this is hysterical. 'Cause they know, like, how people can throb, whole bodies— sometimes I think about gettin' a mastectomy 'cause I don't want anybody to love me for my tits, like oh, man I love your tits wanna suck em man—I don't want anybody sucking my tits. I want—to throb, with some body—a caved-in body, unhuman, love like desperation where you just hold onto one another you just hold on, no, no balls no prick no cunt just holding on, and throbbing—you must like then find out something that nobody else in the world knows.

[Available from New Dramatists]

DANCIN' TO CALLIOPE
by Jack Gilhooley

Shaunelle was once the Kootchie Queen in Barney Harrelson's traveling carnival. She is still attractive and very vain, but has been replaced by her arrogant stepdaughter, Lu Rae. Shaunelle is now the Mermaid, certainly a step down but she still has Ricky, the handsome Half-and-Half on whom her daughter has designs.

An incurable romantic, Shaunelle decries the shabbiness of contemporary carnival life and remembers with love and awe the two people who inspired her in their bizarre but magnetic manner. She relates her story of the Three-Eyed Man and the Bearded Lady to Ricky.

SHAUNELLE (*Animating this like the movie star she always wanted to be*): When I was just a little bitty tadpole, my folks were with Adamo Brothers Starlight International Show. One day, Triclops an' Lucy arrived after they got stranded when American Variety Revue got bankrupt. Well, I figured like you do, that they was just another coupla God's shortchanged people. Y'know, no big deal. Triclops caused a little bit of a stir causa the third eye inna middle of his forehead. Even the veterans, who thought they'd seen everythin' in the way of freaks, were taken a bit aback. Bearded ladies are pretty easy t'come by but three-eyers . . . well, they aren't exactly t'be found on every other street corner. Anyway, everybody adjusted t'them an' they settled in. After a while I started t'become attracted t'them. First thing I noticed was that they never went nowhere without each other. Even when they went t'the ten-in-one. He'd walk 'er t'her booth, then he'd proceed t'his. They'd do their exhibition, then they'd head back t'their trailer hand in hand, just the way they do today. They didn't smoke or drink or do anythin' wrong, an' they had these pretty little flower boxes in alla their windows an' they kept their trailer neat as a pin. They never fought, never cussed each other out, never even raised their voice t'one another. Now, that's rare in carney life, as you'n'I know all too well. An' it's unheard of in the straight world, from what I gather.

Anyways, after a while they started t'ask me t'run errands for 'em. So, I'd go inta the various towns fer them 'cause they didn't wanna leave the grounds. Ya can imagine how the marks woulda reacted iffn the Three-Eyed Man an' the Bearded Lady strolled through the A&P. When I'd return, I'd come t'the front door an' I'd peer through the window an' more often than not, I'd see 'em standin' stark still in one another's arms, right there inna middle of their cheery little livin' room. An' they had this look on their faces—a look that had nothin' to do with the deformity of their faces. The look had t'do with . . . well . . . with ecstasy, I guess. Yeah, ecstasy was what it was. I didn't know at the time what that feelin' was in two people, 'cept from the movies. All I knew was the opposite. All I could draw on was my own experiences, an' whatever the opposite of ecstasy was, my parents had it in spades.

I'd knock onna door an' they'd bring me in an' they'd show me their photo album with their daughter's picture in it. Their daughter was beautiful . . . truly lovely. No third eye . . . no beard . . . just this gorgeous face. They tole me their daughter had run away a little before causa the shame she felt. That made me feel sad. But they weren't bitter—not even hurt, it seemed. They said it was best fer the girl. Can ya imagine that? They said it was God's will an' that they were happy just to have had her. I thought it was funny when they spoke about God. I knew they didn't go to church. I guess they had deeper feelings. I do remember that every day—real early in the mornin' before the townies woke up—they'd stroll off alone t'gether, hand in hand like always, an' toward some secluded spot. One day, I set out t'follow them. The sun hadn't even come up yet, but they had no trouble seein'. Then they raised their hands an' offered up these prayers to God, who I guess was the sun t'them, which was just startin' t'rise. They went fer a good fifteen, twenty minutes, I suppose, sayin' all kindsa prayers that I never heard at any Pentecostal Baptist church. An' every prayer, every last one of 'em, was a prayer of thanksgivin'. Can you imagine that? A prayer of thanksgivin' fer God's bestowed graces!!!

(*Beat.*)

Amazin'! Then as they finished up with a long, loud "Amen," they turned t'one another an' kissed just about the longest kiss I ever did see. Not a soul kiss, y'understand. It was clean an' neat an' warm. Then, like nothin' at all had happened, they turned an' headed back, hand in hand like always. An' I knew beyond a shadow of a doubt, my life would never be quite the same again . . . never again the same.

[Available at New Dramatists]

NAMESAKES
by Amlin Gray

Cilla Hoxie is unmarried and pregnant—she's not sure
by whom. She has just told her mother. It's been hard
news for Leora, but now Cilla has said she's afraid.
All recrimination fades as Leora tries to reassure her
daughter with the story of Cilla's own birth.

LEORA: Don't be frightened, sweetie. I know with
your first baby you're afraid, but don't be. When I had
you—I won't tell you it was easy, but don't be afraid.

I did have drugs. In those days they made everybody take them. But I wouldn't take much. They gave
me ten breaths of the gas, and then half of me watched
while the other half had you. The half that was watching didn't miss a thing. At this point my contractions
were three minutes apart and a minute long, then
longer. "It's nearly ready," said the nurse. "It's going
to come out now, Mrs. Hoxie. You won't stop it now
it's coming, just say yes. Don't push down yet but
don't hold back, and open like it want you to."

You were helping me. You knew what you were
doing. Your head was molding like a boiled egg. It
was stretching me open. The doctor said to help. "Push,"

he said. I lay next to myself and watched my body arching there and pushing, working, every fiber of me working.

Then you crested. In the mirror I could see your head now, round with strands of hair pressed flat and streaming like runnels of water. We were riding your birth like a wave. We strained to catch it—caught it! and we slid together helpless down the curling surface, *russsshhh!* kept sliding and your shoulder then your arm shot out of me, the wave crashed over us, drenched us, slipped back, left us exhausted on the bed. You cried a long cry, breathed, and cried whole lungfuls of new gorgeous noise, and I heard myself say, Oh Christ Jesus, that was *fun!*

You were all there. Nothing missing, nothing out of place. A person from inside me, separate, with unbroken skin all around. You there, there the doctor, there the nurse, and me here, looking at my daughter—who is grown now and who's going to have a baby.

[Contact Lois Berman, 240 W. 44th St., New York, NY 10036]

THE FANTOD
by Amlin Gray

The setting is a young girl's room under the eaves of
an isolated manor house in mid-Victorian England. A
mysterious stranger has come into the life of the household. Sir Tristam Northmoor's experiments make him
frightening to Rachel—and therefore all the more attractive. Rachel is in the throes of her first sensations
of desire. She has locked herself in with her diary.

RACHEL: The spring is at an end already. Something I'll call summer is arriving. When I walk outside,
it all but overwhelms me. Layers of heavy mist en-
shroud the sun. The sky is soaked with heat, as if the
air might burst and sprawl me on my back among the
spongy leaves.

The lilac bushes growing by the west wall spend
their fragrance all across the grounds. Even by the
lake I smell them. In their perfume is an invitation:
"Come to us."

I walk, and as I pass beneath the willow I can see
the lilacs. They are yellow; they smell orange, golden.
They are purple; they smell fiery red. Their emana-
tions come in waves at me. I raise my arms to guard

my face, but the fumes make me reel. I want to throw myself among the banks of lilacs, eat their pale flowers, crush them against my cheeks and eyelids, draw them down by armfuls to my breast—

I know that if I give in to abandon, I will die. I run inside, to the Pavilion Room. Safe here, I ask questions of my plants. About Sir Tristam. Do they answer me?

My special flower folds whenever he approaches. Oh, how well I understand that. I'm afraid of him. I fold just like my flower, but I feel him still. I feel him now, twelve rooms away. He's boiling his herbs. The smell comes wafting through the halls and slides in under the door. Today it smells like lilacs.

[Published by Dramatists Play Service]

LANDSCAPE OF THE BODY
by John Guare

The decapitated body of Betty's son was found down by the docks. Police Captain Marvin Holahan vigorously interrogated her, but Betty refused to confess to the murder of her son. Betty couldn't have killed her son; she was in South Carolina, contemplating marrying Durwood Peach, the man who sold Good Humor ice cream to her when she was a girl. She had left her fourteen-year-old son Bert in New York with one thousand dollars in cash and returned to find him and her lover Raulito dead.

After the police released Betty, she bought a bus ticket to Massachusetts. Now on a ferry boat, looking at the houses of rich and famous families, she meets Captain Holahan and proceeds to explain to him her feelings about Bert's murder.

BETTY: It bothered me at first not knowing who killed Bert. But then I thought of all the things we don't know. All the secrets in the world got put in a bottle and thrown in the sea, and maybe someday I'll be walking along a beach and the bottle containing the message for me will wash up. If I don't know the answer, it's there and one day maybe an incredible coincidence will occur and I'll know all I need to know. Or the murderer will come forward. Or I'll even forget once I had a secret. I'll remember I had a boy like I'll remember I once had a mother and once had a father, and I'll try to keep piling the weight on the present, so I'll stay alive and won't slide back. If I don't know, somebody knows. My life is a triumph of all the things I don't know. I don't have to know everything. I read Agatha Christies and throw them away when the detective says, "And the murderer is . . ." The mystery's always greater than the solution. I was terrified to have a kid. I said before I got pregnant, I'll have a kid and the eyes will end up on one side of the face and all the fingers on one hand and all the toes on one foot and both ears on one side of the head. And Bert was born and he was perfect. And this is the only thing I know. There's got to be some order in there. I'm moving to this new place and it has big houses with classical columns and maybe I'll find a job in one of them in a house owned by an old man who has an art collection and I'll read up on classical painters and maybe he'll ask me to marry him or maybe I'll kill him and get him to sign the collection over to me or maybe I'll love him and marry him. Or maybe I'll discover a secret inside me that will make the whole world better. I'm not discounting nothing. Maybe I'll be transplanted into somebody great who knows the secret, my secret, or maybe I'll never know and a tornado or a water spout will whisk me up and I'll turn into rain and end up in the sea.

[Published by Harcourt Brace Jovanovich]

THE HOUSE OF BLUE LEAVES
by John Guare

Bananas is a nervous woman who's lived in her nightgown for the last six months. She's in her early forties and has been crying for as long as she's had her nightgown on. She is married to Artie Shaughnessy, a man who loves her but feels weighed down by her. She is afraid Artie is going to put her in a home. After Artie has announced that he's going to seek his fortune in California with the woman who lives downstairs, Bananas describes the dream/fantasy that led her to go up to the roof of her building, wearing nothing but a nightgown, on a cold winter night.

BANANAS: My troubles all began a year ago—two years ago today—two days ago today? Today.

We used to have a beautiful old green Buick. The Green Latrine! . . . I'm not allowed to drive it anymore . . . but when I could drive it . . . the last time I drove it, I drove into Manhattan.

And I drive down Broadway—to the Crossroads of the World.

I see a scene that you wouldn't see in your wildest

dreams. Forty-second Street. Broadway. Four corners. Four people. One on each corner. All waving for taxis. Cardinal Spellman. Jackie Kennedy. Bob Hope. President Johnson. All carrying suitcases. Taxi! Taxi! I stop in the middle of the street—the middle of Broadway—and I get out of my Green Latrine and yell, "Get in. I'm a gypsy. A gypsy cab. Get in. I'll take you where you want to go. Don't you all know each other? Get in. Get in!"

They keep waving for cabs. I run over to President Johnson and grab him by the arm. "Get in!" And pull Jackie Kennedy into my car and John-John, who I didn't see, starts crying and Jackie hits me and I hit her and I grab Bob Hope and push Cardinal Spellman into the back seat, crying and laughing, "I'll take you where you want to go. Get in! Give me your suitcases"—and the suitcases spill open and Jackie Kennedy's wigs blow down Forty-second Street and Cardinal Spellman hits me and Johnson screams and I hit him. I hit them all. And then the Green Latrine blows four flat tires and sinks and I run to protect the car and four cabs appear and all my friends run into four different cabs. And the cars are honking for me to move.

I push the car over the bridge back to Queens. You're asleep. I turn on Johnny Carson to get my mind off and there's Cardinal Spellman and Bob Hope, whose nose is still bleeding, and they tell the story of what happened to them and everybody laughs. Thirty million people watch Johnny Carson and they all laugh. At me. I'm nobody. I knew all those people better than me. You. Ronnie. I know everything about them. Why can't they love me?

And then it began to snow and I went up on the roof . . .

[Published by Viking Press]

NIGHT LUSTER
by Laura Harrington

Roma is a singer/songwriter in her twenties who keeps getting used and abused by her men. In this monologue, Roma is speaking to her best friend, Mink, a call girl. Roma lives off love and hope even though it's Mink, rather than the men in her life, who understands her.

ROMA: I don't think people see me. I get this feeling sometimes like I'm invisible or something. I can be standing there in a room and I'm talking and everything, and it's like my words aren't getting anywhere and I look down at myself and *jesus,* sometimes my body isn't getting anywhere either. It's like I'm standing behind a one-way mirror and I can see the guys and I can hear the guys, but they can't see me and they can't hear me. And I start to wonder if maybe I'm ugly or something, like maybe I'm some alien species from another planet and I don't speak the language and I look totally weird. But I don't know this, you see, because on this other planet I had this really nice mother who told me I was beautiful and that I had a voice to die for because she loved me so much, not because it was true. And I arrive here on earth and I'm so filled with her love and her belief in me that I walk around like I'm beautiful and I sing like I have a voice to die for. And because I'm so *convinced* and so strange and so *deluded*, people *pretend* to listen to me . . . because they're being polite or something—or maybe they're afraid of me. And at first I don't notice because I sing with my eyes closed. But then one day I open my eyes and I find out I'm living in this world where nobody sees me and nobody hears me.

(*Beat.*)

I'm just lookin' for that one guy who's gonna hear *me,* see *me* . . . really take a chance. I mean, I hear *them.* I'm listening so hard I hear promises when somebody's just sayin' hello.

Jesus, if anybody ever heard what I've got locked up inside of me . . . I'd be a *star.*

[Available at New Dramatists]

COME BACK, LITTLE SHEBA
by William Inge

Lola is a worn, disheveled, disillusioned housewife. She desperately craves companionship, especially male companionship (her husband Doc is an ex-alcoholic). She used to own a puppy name Sheba, but it ran away, leaving her alone while her husband works. This morning she tries to persuade the postman to sit and chat for a while to momentarily alleviate the oppressive boredom of her life.

LOLA: You postmen have things pretty nice, don't you? I hear you get nice pensions after you been working for the government twenty years. I think that's dandy. It's a good job, too. You may be tired, but I think it's good for a man to be outside and get a lot of exercise. Keeps him strong and healthy. My husband, he's a doctor, a *chiro*practor; he has to stay inside his office all day long. The only exercise he gets is rubbin' peoples' backbones. It makes his hands strong. He's got the strongest hands you ever did see. But he's got poor digestion. I keep tellin' him he oughta get some fresh air once in a while and some exercise.

(*The* POSTMAN *rises to go, and this hurries her into a more absorbing monologue.*)

You know what? My husband is an Alcoholics Anonymous. He doesn't care if I tell you that 'cause he's proud of it. He hasn't touched a drop in almost a year. All that time we've had a quart of whiskey in the pantry for company, and he hasn't even gone near it. Doesn't even want to. You know, alcoholics can't drink like ordinary people; they're allergic to it. It affects them different. They get started drinking and can't stop. Liquor transforms them. Sometimes they get mean and violent and want a fight—but if they let liquor alone, they're perfectly all right, just like you and me.

(POSTMAN *tries to leave.*)

You should have seen Doc before he gave it up. He lost all his patients, wouldn't even go to the office; just wanted to stay drunk all day long and he'd come home at night and . . . You just wouldn't believe it if you saw him now. He's got his patients all back, and he's just doing fine.

You don't ever drink, do you?

[Published by Grove Press]

MOVING
by Lee Kalcheim

Megan is a tough, sexy young woman starting her life in New York. She tells her best friend Diana a story that only goes to show Diana that Megan has been much the same since she was a little girl.

MEG: Can you imagine a combination more deadly than a Jewish mother and an Irish Catholic father? One giveth and the other taketh away.

Can you imagine me in church? It wasn't easy. You know what my biggest problem was? I thought I was smarter than all the priests. I had to hear those dumb, dumb sermons. Y'know, where the theme would be something like, "Be good to your mother." I used to wise-ass in Sunday school. Finally, one of the priests called me in and said, "Shea? What's your problem?" I said, "My problem is that I don't believe any of this bullshit." I didn't say bullshit to the priest—I said something like, "stuff." "I don't believe any of this stuff." He said, "What is it you don't believe?" I said, "Take your pick." So he started, "Do you believe in the Father?" I said, "No." "The son?" "No." "The Holy Ghost?" "No." "Do you believe in anything?" That's when I said, "Yes . . . confession." "How can you believe in confession?" I said, " 'Cause it's a great idea. It predates Freud by twelve centuries."

So I left the Church. Quit Catholic school. Mom figured I was making a leap to Judaism. I told her. "Mom. I don't believe in God in three places and I don't believe in God in one place. Religion's a crutch. I'm not gonna substitute one crutch for another." Then my mother says—dig this—she says, "Megan, my child. Everybody's gotta have a crutch. Everybody has to have a god. You don't want a Jewish god? You want a Catholic god? You'll have a god someday. Believe me."

Well . . . if she's not right, she certainly kept me on my toes, because there isn't a day that goes by that I don't wake up and wonder if I'm going to find a god today.

In this second monologue, Diana, fresh out of college, has moved into her first, depressing New York apartment, a long way from her upper-class Philadelphia upbringing. She explains to her best friend, Megan, her conflicting feelings about this past, particularly her mother.

DIANA: I went to a Quaker school. Absolutely *un*competitive! We used to have an awards ceremony at the end of the year. Everybody got an award! Then it dawned on me that if everybody got an award, it didn't mean anything . . . So I went to the headmaster and I told him, "Why don't you give up the awards altogether. I mean, if everybody gets an award, it doesn't mean anything." He looked at me and said, "Diana, not everyone realizes that. There are boys and girls here who have never ever gotten an award in their life. It means something to them. So for that reason, we do it." And I said, "But don't you realize how condescending that is to them? It's ultimately going to make them feel worse." He just glared at me and said, "Miss Schmidt. Someday, somebody's going to prick your bubble." I just . . . I couldn't help it. I burst out laughing. So he called my mother.

She came into school. Came in looking like a million dollars. Camel's hair coat. Blonde hair. Looked like a Smith College undergrad. Came in smelling like an ocean breeze. I looked at her and said to myself, "I'm gonna get it." Mr. Dumwalt, the headmaster, told her what I said . . . and Mom took me aside. She sat me down . . . and said, "Don't worry about Mr. Dumwalt. He was born with a pole up his ass!" I couldn't believe it. I think that's one of the reasons I've never abandoned hope for Mom.

[Available at New Dramatists]

THE WALL OF WATER
by Sherry Kramer

The Mosquito Bite

Wendi is a woman who was once wonderful and who has been making a gradual, painful descent into madness. She has been under a doctor's care and heavy-maintenance medication for many years. She is awakened by a mosquito bite on a day when she is wavering between a semblance of normalcy and yet another plunge into the abyss.

WENDI (*Tracks the passage of a mosquito buzzing about her head. She may indeed make the buzzing noise. She slaps at it.*): I imagine a world completely pestilence-ridden. The slightest touch, the smallest bruise, will blossom and decay. I imagine bank lines stretching for miles, and none of the tellers caring, and all of the people in the line oozing and bleeding from arms and legs and faces covered with open sores and scabs. Piebald from rashes. I imagine great armies of mosquitoes preying upon these people, wafting down on them in swarms that quite cloud the sky. They suck and sting their way up and down the line, spreading the pestilence, a thousand separate plagues, from one pockmarked, stinking carrier to the next, the bills and bank cards in their hands soaked and slimy with death and disease. Suddenly the attack is called off. The cloud of mosquitoes rises, riding the city thermals up and up. And one of them . . . one of them . . . one of them floats inside my open window. I mean to keep it closed. I mean to keep it closed, but I forget. It comes in my window, and it bites me. *It bites me.* And it carries in its bite a hundred horrible plagues and all of them will deform me hideously while I die.

(*The mosquito begins buzzing her again.* WENDI *slaps, claps at it desperately. She gets it. She holds it triumphantly between her finger and her thumb.*)

Gotcha.

The Wall of Water
The Last Cigarette

Meg is a woman who always obeys her own golden rule: Never stomp on anybody weaker than you are. Stomp on anybody stronger than you are, if you can. She has recently moved into a wonderful apartment, but discovered almost immediately, and to her horror, that one of the roommates is completely, irretrievably insane. This roommate has subjected Meg to countless tiny tragedies. But Meg has never raised her voice, or in any way defended herself, because she knows that the roommate is sick, and therefore weak—too weak for her to be able to strike back.

This monologue finds Meg on the morning she has decided that she cannot hold back a moment longer. She must convince herself that her insane roommate is in fact the stronger, and therefore justify her striking back.

MEG (*She lights up a cigarette, the last in the pack.*): Did you ever notice how the sound of the hot water changes when it gets hot? I did.

I noticed a lot of other things, besides.

One day I woke up and noticed that most of those things made me angry.

Then I noticed something else.

That if I took a long, hot shower, I wasn't angry anymore.

Then I had a lot of thoughts, all at once. Thoughts like, what if the water shortage gets really bad. What if the boiler breaks, and stays broken for a long time, and all my friends are out of town, and all the hotel rooms are full. What if Adolf Hitler had taken more hot showers. What if he did, and it didn't help. What if one day I took a long hot shower, and I was still very angry about a lot of things when I came out.

(MEG *smiles.*)

What if I'm going to take that shower now. What if I've already taken it, and don't know. What if I'm getting angrier and angrier and they could heat up the Canadian side of Niagara Falls to the boiling point, keep the American side running cold, put handles on the side, throw me a big bar of soap, and it still wouldn't calm me down. What then?

Because you know why I'm angry? You really want to know?

My roommate Wendi steals my cigarettes. She steals my cigarettes and it creates a rage in me greater and more terrifying than the rage created in me by the thought of early death caused by many forms of cancer, even though I don't have any of them and even if I did they could be diagnosed in time and I could probably be saved. Unless it was head cancer. Or throat cancer. Or lung cancer.

(MEG *stamps out her cigarette.*)

Which I also do not stand a good chance of getting, if I stop.

But that's not why I'm going to stop.

I am going to stop because when Wendi steals my cigarettes, she doesn't steal all of them. She steals all of them but one.

I take it only as a sign of the influence of a civilization on even the criminally insane that Wendi never takes my last one. It has nothing to do with consideration. Compassion. Courtesy. Wendi has left all those things far behind. Trains can't stop her. Bullets can't stop her. She threatens to leap from tall buildings in a single bound. Medical science can't help her. Deep hypnosis can't reach her. But the myth of the last cigarette stops her. Dead, every time.

If she would just take the last cigarette, maybe I wouldn't be so angry. But no, she takes nineteen and stops. She opens a fresh pack, empties them all out, and replaces one.

I want to kill Wendi.

(*Pause.*)

Or maybe I'll just take a shower instead.

[Available at New Dramatists]

SPLIT SECOND
by Dennis McIntyre

The story is a simple one. A policeman named Val
shoots a suspect in a burglary. The policeman is black,
the victim, white. Against the advice of his retired
policeman father, his best friend on the force, his wife,
Alea, and everyone else he confronts, the black policeman cannot come to grips with simply lying and
letting the matter rest.

ALEA: You're alive, aren't you? Who cares about
the truth anymore? Who ever did? Unless they got
caught. What's the truth mean, anyway? You recited
his record. He was a pimp. He was a hustler. He was a
thief. He smuggled cigarettes from North Carolina.
He went to prison in New York. He went to prison in
Michigan. He carried a knife, and if you'd given him
the chance, he probably would have killed you. That's
your fucking truth, Val. But he was white. Don't you
ever forget that. White! You tell them what really
happened, and they'll crucify you. And not just you.
Me. All of us. The next black man who wants to be a
cop, you think they're not going to think twice about
giving him a gun? The next black kid they blow away

in Bed-Sty, you don't think they're going to bring up your name? Because when black people pull the trigger, that's not insanity, that's spontaneity! Give the gorilla a banana, he's going to eat it! And I'll tell you one thing, Val Johnson, you go to prison, you won't survive it. The guards are going to hate you. You're the ex-cop who couldn't control himself. The whites are going to hate you. You're the ex-black cop who couldn't control himself. "Control," Val! Remember? But the blacks, they're going to hate you most of all. And do you want to know why? Out of contempt, that's why! Contempt! Why'd you have to go and let them know?

Keep that in mind tomorrow morning, and keep asking yourself the other question—"Where are we going to be?!"

[Published by Samuel French]

BLUE MOON
by Grace McKeaney

Winnie Noble is a healer and spiritualist in her mid-forties. Winnie is a plainspoken woman who calls a spade a spade. A psychic, she possesses the ability to establish intimate relationships with everyone she meets, clearly seeing their destinies. Winnie is speaking to the world in these two monologues.

WINNIE: I was raised in Noble, Kansas. I'm a Noble and somehow the Nobles managed to hold fast in that shifting landscape an unlikely long time. Kansas ain't the easiest place to hold your head up, but we're stubborn. And the rest of them will be there as long as it takes to get through their lives, but not me. I won't never go back to Kansas. Not since I've learned to float.

My mama brought me to the Boardwalk all the way from Kansas when I was a child of six, just to see the water . . . She suffered always with dreams of water . . . that's 'cause she was going to die in the water . . . And now the water is my shadow, too. Got to be by it, hear it lapping. And once you learned to lie on your back and float, which is important in this here life, you got to stay by the water so's you don't get out of practice.

Don't get me wrong. Kansas is okay. It's easy to find on a map. It's there in the middle of everything getting beat daily by the wind, and there are folks like the people I'm from that thrive on standing up to it. But I got my fill of the wind whipping folks like the devil whipped his children. Got my fill of long, dry days and lonesome shadows on prairie afternoons.

I like the ocean because you can't cut it with a knife no matter how hard you try. It's all of a piece and I like that. What I feel is there's no place good or bad of its own. Where you wind up depends purely on your nature and, of course, on what's in store for you.

WINNIE: Now here's an interesting thing about me: I lost my hearing in a dust storm when I was newly born. Spent my precious childhood as deaf as a stone. What's the difference? Most folks hear what they want to. I heard as much ever as I needed. Folks, as a rule, don't have a powerful lot that needs saying. You can see all you need to, if you got eyes.

As it happened, this one summer my daddy didn't love my mama no more. Nobody ever had to say a thing to me about it. Some things you know.

She knew. She knew he wouldn't come back this time. I seen the careful way she took his clean clothes from the line that morning. I seen the way the wind made the wash smack her in the face like just everything was against her. I seen the way she hung back, then run after him into the barn. And I seen through the window how she clung to his leg like a child.

Now I don't know what use that was. He was going. All that was left was his body riding off. His heart rode off from that place years before only Mama was too proud to *see*.

I knew all this because my daddy showed me things I guess he shouldn't have. Sunday, Mama would teach Sunday school, teaching one and all how everything had a season, and I got something useful out of that. But it was Saturdays when Daddy would take me to the matinee movies that I saw what life held when its season was ripe in bloom. My daddy loved the ladies in the movies more even than the cowboys. He had a eye for gold. The ones with the yellow hair like the wheat waving there behind our barn, they were his particular fancy. Gayla had yellow hair.

Gayla run the feed store across from the moving-picture house. And in time, Gayla and my daddy kinda struck it up. For good. Daddy would drop a handful of gumdrops in my apron, and I'd sit on Gayla's stoop after the movie and watch them change the letters on the marquee and chew my gumdrops and wait for them two to finish up. And sometimes they didn't get it done till the last gumdrop was gone. My daddy and Gayla was always making plans for how they were going to be happy someday, and my daddy's whole restless attitude left him when he was rolling up a Viceroy there at her little table. 'Way he looked at her after finishing a meal she made him was like he was still hungry . . . but not in a starving, grasping way. More like the sweet, thorough way a dragonfly draws sweetness from a flower . . . My daddy loved this lady in a deep and thorough way and I guess as far as I was concerned, I didn't mind the gumdrops.

My daddy never let on to Mama. He didn't have to. She knew even if she couldn't see. Mama's hair was black as silt and stick-straight. And that was not her fault. She was always glad of my yellow hair and I always been glad of it, too. What a trick of nature to think you could lose a husband or a daddy depending on which way your hair went. I guess you could say life had left us very realistic. When my daddy left us. And we came to California.

[Available at New Dramatists]

A NARROW BED
by Ellen McLaughlin

Megan is a woman in her late thirties or early forties whose husband has been missing in action in Vietnam for fifteen years. She still harbors some hope that he is alive. She tells her friend Lucy about the only sexual experience she has had since he left.

MEGAN: There was this guy I saw waiting for a bus. He . . . well, I was really shocked. He looked a lot, I mean *a lot* like John. I saw him from across the street. I was holding all these groceries and I just stood there staring at him like a crazy person. He didn't know I was watching him because he was doing this—well, actually, this very John thing, as a matter of fact—he was reading the back of his ticket. That's just what John used to do—he'd read things, the wrappers on candy bars, airplane safety folders, baggage tickets . . . Anyway, the guy didn't notice me. But I just couldn't move. I knew it wasn't John, but I couldn't seem to convince myself. There was this child in me, this little girl jumping up and down saying, "It's him, it's him, he's come back!" Finally I did this thing. I crossed the street and I went up to him. I said, "Excuse me, but I have a sort of unusual request. I'll pay for that ticket, wherever you're going, if you would sit and talk with me for a few minutes." He said, "You'd pay for a ticket to Chicago just to talk?" and I said, "You're right, it's not just to talk. You'd have to kiss me." He said something like "What is this?" and then I told him. I showed him a picture of John. He saw the likeness. He even vaguely knew someone who was also missing-in-action . . . Anyway . . . anyway, I asked him to come out with me someplace. We turned in the ticket. It was all pretty weird, actually . . . So, yeah, we made love. Yeah. I got my diaphragm out of the crypt and everything. (*Laughs.*) Jesus, I mean, this poor guy. I don't know why he did it—I'm sure he regretted it as soon as we decided to. And he's trying to deal with *me* and I can't even *look* at him. He probably felt like a stud. A bad stud at that. I kept crying. (MEGAN *is laughing.*)

Oh God. (*She recovers.*) Yeah . . . I sometimes wonder what's happened to him, you know, whether he's all right about it now. You know, turned it into a funny story, or whether he did what I did—buried it.

That was, oh, I don't know, about five years ago. That was the only time. Yeah, that was it.

[Available at New Dramatists]

ON THE VERGE or THE GEOGRAPHY OF YEARNING
by Eric Overmyer

Mary is a veteran explorer and a passionate, life-loving woman. She is a scientist, but not dry or dull; she has a scientist's ebullient curiosity. She is from Boston, but doesn't have a Boston accent. Her yearning is the most intense of the three women who have decided to embark on an expedition into Terra Incognita in 1888. Mary rejoices at the prospect of traveling through time and space in this monologue.

MARY: The splash of galaxies across the night sky always brings out the phenomenologist in me.

Billions of new worlds waiting to be discovered. Explored and illuminated. Within and without. The nautilus shell mimics the shape of the Milky Way. Quarks and quasars. My face is bathed in light from a vanished star.

(*Beat.*)

I stand at the precipice. The air is rare. Bracing. Before me stretch dark distances. Clusters of light.

What next? I have no idea. Many mysteries to come. I am on the verge.

(MARY *surveys the horizon and her prospects.*)

I have a yearning for the future! It is boundless! (*She takes a deep breath.*) Not annoying. Not annoying at all!

In this second monologue, Alex is an intelligent young explorer who feels out of place in the Victorian world. She enjoys examining things and looking at old things in a new light. As she journeys through time, she eagerly embraces the future with loving arms.

ALEX (*Taking a deep breath*): The rare air of the future. Breathe. Aspirate. Aspire. A-spire. (ALEX *takes another deep breath.*) One of the ecstasies of hiking in the Himalayas was to crest a ridge, and suddenly confront the infinite surround. Mountains and rivers without end. Untouched. Glistening with possibility. We are climbing a spire of time. The topography of the future is coming into view. Unmapped and unnamed. Distant vistas shining. You must not shrink. You must embrace it with all your heart.

[Published by Broadway Play Publishing Company]

MARY GOLDSTEIN
by OyamO (Charles F. Gordon)

Because of an earlier violent argument with her husband, Arnold, that morning, Mary Goldstein, quintessential housewife and sensitive closet poet, has decided to spend the day reciting and acting out her own poetry for herself. She uses the playroom and the children's toys as set and props. The following passage is a kind of narrative of the circumstances surrounding her engagement and wedding. It is an attempt to rediscover happier moments and to understand just how she trapped herself, due to social expectations, into a marriage immediately after high school.

(MARY *swirls about to a lovely dance tune, picks up a small purse and a hand bouquet of plastic flowers. After joyfully dancing a bit, she speaks:*)

MARY: Oh, Arnold, I had such a beauuutiful time at the senior prom tonight. This has been one night that I'll never forget. Arnold, we shouldn't wake up your brother and his wife. It's so late. They asked you to bring me by? To see us in our prom outfits? That's sweet. Oh, you have a key, your brother lets you have a key to his house? . . Oh, just for tonight.

(*Steps inside.*)

Oh, Arnold, you'd better wake them now so we can get going.

(MARY *walks around humming to herself, picking a bit of lint off her "dress," smoothing and brushing where appropriate—"Arnold" returns.*)

They're not in? Why would they go out when they knew we were coming? Hey, Arnold, why are you taking off your shoes and your jacket? . . . You want to rest for a minute? Oh, Arnold, couldn't we just rest at my house? . . . You don't want to wake my parents? But how would we wake them if we're only resting? . . . Oh, Arnold, what are you doing? . . . Taking off my shoes? . . . I know you're taking off my shoes, but I want to know why . . . (*Suddenly whoops and wildly kicks out her legs.*) Oh Arnold, you're tickling me! Stop it! Arnold!

(*Calms.*)

See there, you know I'm ticklish on my feet. Arnold, why are you on your knees in front of me? . . . You want to rub my tired little feet? . . . Oh how sweet, but don't tickle me, you hear? . . . Oh Arnold, what are you doing?

(*Suddenly whoops and pushes his "hands" off her knees.*) See there, that's unfair. You know my knees are also ticklish . . . Oh Arnold, don't feel discouraged; you can still rub my feet if you want to . . . there. Isn't this nice and cozy . . . Oh Arnold, no, baby . . . Oh Arnold, no, baby . . . Oh Arnold, Arnold, Arnold . . .

(MARY *"kicks" him solidly upside the head.*)

Oh Arnold, I didn't mean to hurt you . . . I'm sorry
. . . Honest . . . It was just the way you were licking
my knees; it made me have a muscle spasm . . . Huh?
. . . Did I like it? Oh, spasms are all right, I suppose; I
. . . Oh, you mean did I like the licking?

(*Giggles.*)

Oh Arnold, no, I hated it. I mean the tickling; the
licking was soothing . . . Well, we better be going now
. . . Arnold, please don't . . . No, No, No!

(*Her whole body convulses backward, away from
"Arnold."*) Oh Arnold, your hands are all the way up
to my other places . . . I can't stand it, your hands
are so hot . . . Oh Arnold, no, no, baby, please,
no . . .

(*With one mighty heave of her whole body,* MARY
*"throws" him off, shakes her head violently as if shak-
ing off a spell, and says firmly in a convincing show of
mock anger but with a sense of victory:—*)

Arnold, we have to wait until we're married like we
said . . . (*Then, softly.*) Oh, baby, I want you, too . . . I
know it don't make no difference, but we promised to
wait . . . How long? . . . We should wait at least until
the wedding date has been set . . . You want to set a
date now? . . . Let's see, that would make the date
June 23. O.K. Is this what *you* really want, Arnold?
Then I accept because what you want is what I want
. . . Oh Arnold, you've made me so happy tonight
. . . Oh Arnold, your fingers are so strong . . . Arnold, don't tear my dress . . Oh Arnold, baby, baby,
baby, yes, yes, baby . . . Oh Arnold . . .

[Available at New Dramatists]

A BAG OF GOODIES
by Allan Rieser

A neatly dressed, jolly-looking lady in her sixties, who could not possibly be mistaken for a bag lady, is sitting on a brightly colored plastic seat in a bus depot, rummaging patiently and purposefully in an outsized, shapeless traveling bag which she shifts about from time to time. She appears at first glance to be simply a nice grandmother like many another, yet after a bit her almost ritualistic motions and her look of intensely focused benevolence suggest something more—a figure out of myth, a beaming, bespectacled, undistractible Fate; one might easily imagine that the objects she keeps rearranging in her bag are small, packaged human destinies, given into her charge by a divine will with whom she is on perfect terms. That this fancy is not too fanciful we soon learn as she strikes up a cheery conversation with another traveler who, although invisible to the audience, is seated among them.

WOMAN: Pardon me, young lady—was that the bus for Boston they just called out? . . . I didn't think it could be yet. Is that the one you're getting, too? . . . Oh, good. Then I'll just keep my eye on you . . . One, two, three, four . . . If I talk to myself, don't-pay any attention, please.

I have all these knitting projects underway—one for each member of the family—and sometimes I lose track for a minute.

I have fifteen in all, scattered right across the country—three daughters and their husbands and nine grandchildren.

By rights I should have left five sweaters in Kansas City, but my visit was cut short before I could finish them. Now the children's things will all have to be a size larger. Never mind. When they shout "Gramsy!" and throw their little arms around my neck it makes all my fussin' worthwhile!

Of course, Janet's kids are a little upset right now. Janet is my middle daughter—the one I was just stayin' with in Kansas City. If I'd a-had just a little more time there I could've straightened it all out. Not that I know everything, mind. As I said when my husband died and the girls decided to take me for four months—I told them flat out, I said, "I'm never goin' to give any of you a word of advice, come whatever." And I've stuck by it religiously.

That's why it surprised me so when Janet turned on me. Oh, my, what a tantrum! Locking herself in her room and throwing shoes at the door. Lord knows, I don't have a thing against Joe—her husband, that is. But when a person has a problem, it's no favor pretendin' you don't see.

My son-in-law is a teacher, but he smokes marijuana —pot, as you young folks call it. Only at home on weekends—so Janet says. All I know is, I do recognize that sickly sweet smell. Oof!

Well, while I was there, the PTA called a big meeting—everybody came, kids and all, to talk about drugs. And Julie—Janet's oldest—she come to me beforehand. Julie said some of the kids were goin' to report on their parents, and did I think she should, too. Well, I hope the day never comes when I'm afraid to stand up for the right.

Naturally, it all come home to me. Janet called it spite. She said I've always had it in for Joe because he's a poor breadwinner. She even claimed he might lose his job.

"Fiddlesticks!" I told her. "Nobody fires teachers—even when they can't speak English."

I just hope some good comes of it all.

I'm goin' on now to my oldest daughter's, in Quincy, Massachusetts. They're takin' me in for an extra month to fill in the gap. Ruth has always been the saint of the family. She has to be, with that husband of hers, and his eye for young women.

But for now, mum's the word. I don't want Ruth mad at me, too. And Jean, out in Pasadena, she's still a little miffed because I said Wally liked his martinis too much . . . Oh, they'll all get over it. They know their kids won't ever be happy without Gramsy—and her bag of goodies . . . Well, if you could give me a hand as far as the bus, I'd be grateful. Seems everywhere I go there's a kind young lady to help me . . .

[Available at New Dramatists]

SOUVENIRS
by Sheldon Rosen

Mrs. Harold is in her late seventies and is completing a final trip around the world that will bring her home to Boulder City in Australia after being away for fifty years. The monologue is being delivered to those sitting with her at her table in the dining room of the Hotel Paradisio as they are being filmed by the hotel manager for a holiday travelogue.

MRS. HAROLD: We were living in Boulder City at the time. Outside Perth. Hannah Street, named after a Mr. Hannah. Father had a major gold mine there. Whenever we had guests, he would give them a large nugget as a souvenir. Worth nothing then, but can you imagine?

Anyway, I was an absolute child at the time. This very intense young man, Oscar, was quite in love with me. And although infatuated with the whole idea, I was not quite willing to go against my parents. Oscar wanted to marry me, but my mother would have none of it. Oscar felt that if he couldn't have me, then no one would have me. I think he must have had quite a bit to drink that night; he might have even been on something; he was very odd. He asked me for a drive. I should have been suspicious, but I think I was attracted to the feeling that things were not in my own hands. We were in the back and his driver was in front, but with the glass closed you really can't hear a thing in the front. Oscar was getting quite excited by this time and I wasn't at all sure what he was talking about. I didn't expect passion to be so incoherent. I guess I expected some kind of heightened lucidity, some sense of vision to it. Suddenly he had his hands on my throat. I thought he was joking at first, but he wouldn't stop. It was certainly proper to object at that point, but I was quite dizzy by then. Fortunately, the driver noticed and stopped the car and pulled me away. I think Oscar passed out then. Anyway, the driver—Arthur was his name, a sweet man, truly—gave me a chocolate, which, although I adore, was very hard to swallow because of my throat, and he drove me safely home. After that, Oscar used to follow me all the time. Wherever I'd go, he'd be following on the opposite side of the street. It was quite frightening, actually. Mother hired a private detective to go with me everywhere. One day Mother and I were out walking and Mother was looking in a shop window when a car backfired and she nearly had heart failure on the spot thinking I'd been shot. The next week we moved to Melbourne.

[Available at New Dramatists]

NIBS
by June Septant (Sydney Chandler)

Miss Marvel is an outrageous old pirate, a fortyish American entertainer caught in the London Blitz, swaggering around in her old Patou gowns, her cigarette holder at the ready. Her London club has just been bombed.

MISS MARVEL: I should have known they would never let us have any fun! I've never met a Nazi with a sense of humor. Well, never mind, if you would give me your arm. I feel as though I need a pair of crutches. There will always be an England, but I must admit that London seems to be getting too bloody hot for me. I have the feeling that "someone up there" is trying to tell me something. I'm ready to book passage on anything short of a tin tub for the States. If there's a travel agent left in London, I'll find him. Damn the torpedoes—full speed ahead! is what I say! Lose a battle. Win a war. Well, all my grand illusions have gone up in smoke, literally. It's really a joke, but I'm still alive, and what more can one want really, except to be mistress of one's fate, which I still surely am, no less so than before. After all, the name of the game now is survival, keeping alive, for which I've had more than a few years' experience. I'll have to play it as it lays now—see what fabulous surprises lie ahead. Life. Is there a more exciting game in town?

[Available at New Dramatists]

the dreamer examines his pillow
by John Patrick Shanley

Donna is an intense girl who's been having some trouble with her boyfriend, Tommy. And she's just discovered that Tommy may be a lot like her father, whom she hasn't seen in years. Having a boyfriend who is like her father is exactly what Donna has been trying to avoid. So, to sort things out, Donna visits Dad.

DONNA: A really lousy picture, self-portrait. But it scared me. I think more than anything that's ever happened to me. I heard the fuckin Twilight Zone music. Cause here I am goin along, thinkin things are one way, that I'm choosin an goin my own way, an maybe doin a terrible fuckin botch a that, but doin it. An then I see this picture. And I think, Do I really know what's goin on in my life? Or am I just a complete molecule or some shit. If this guy Tommy is turnin into you, then I'm in some kinda car I don't even know I'm in, and some guy inna scary mask is drivin, and he's had the route the map since the doctor smacked my ass. Where am I? I'm in love with this guy Tommy. He's drivin' me crazy, yeah. He's tearin my heart out and steppin on it, yes. The whole thing I'm doin looks to be a total fuckup, but I can deal with that, I can live with that. But what I wanna know gotta know is *Is this my life or what?* Is this my pain? My love? Or is what's goin on here just like history? You treated my mother like shit. You cheated on her. You lied to her. You humiliated her in public. When you had money, you wouldn't give her any. When she had money, you took it. You walked on her face with muddy shoes. When she was in the hospital, you didn't visit her. And then finally she just fuckin died. Now, I hate your fuckin guts for that, but I decided a long time since that I wasn't gonna spend my whole life wishin you dead or different, cause I didn't want my life bossed by your life. I even thought, Maybe she deserved it. I knew I didn't know the whole story and never would an what was it my business anyway? But that was before. Today, I saw that picture on Tommy's wall, an it was writin on the wall to me, an the writin said, Watch Out. You could be in the middle of somebody else's life. So that's why I'm here. Because before I thought I didn't have to know bout you to do my life, and now I see I better find out a few things. It's like medical history.

[Published by Dramatists Play Service]

MORTALLY FINE
by William J. Sibley

Mary Nell Hubka is a middle-aged, thrice-divorced Texas heiress. After the demise of her most recent husband, Irv Leibowitz (in a fall from the stage of the Las Vegas Dunes during "The Mitzi Gaynor Show") she inherits twenty million dollars and returns to her hometown to reclaim her true love, Elvin Shoemaker.

In this scene, she recounts the tale of her brief marriage to Irv. Mary Nell is tough, shrewd, funny—a survivor.

MARY NELL: Irv and I were still on our honeymoon in Las Vegas when he fell off the stage at the Dunes and broke his neck. During "The Mitzi Gaynor Show." She's so darlin' that Mitzi. She'll never see fifty again, but honey, she's got a figure a high school girl would envy. I've always been a big fan of Mitzi's.

(*Beat.*)

In a way I guess it's my fault Irv fell off the stage. He wanted to go over to the Sands and catch Shecky Green and I said, "Oh, no, if there's no singing and dancing and pretty girls in feathers and jewels, I'm just not interested."

(*Beat.*)

Well, Mitzi's got this little number in her act where she invites a couple of men in the audience to join her in a conga line. It's real cute. And I just insisted Irv get up cause I'd brought my little Instamatic to take pictures. Honey, that conga line grew longer and longer and wilder and wilder, and Mitzi's just tearing around the stage like a cat with her tail on fire. I'm standing on my chair trying to find Irv in the viewfinder and next thing I know, all hell breaks loose. There's seventy-one-year-old Irving Leibowitz on the tail end of the world's longest conga line swinging around in front of the orchestra going forty miles an hour. Last thing I saw was my husband waving at me as he flew over the table wearing a grass skirt and one of Mitzi's earrings. All I could think was, "Shalom, y'all, it's been fun."

(*Beat.*)

Naturally, Irv's lawyer and I sued Mitzi and her raggedy-ass little show. Sued the Dunes for negligence. Sued the city of Las Vegas for permitting such sordid entertainment to go on in the first place . . . oh, it was real pleasant.

So I'm back in Houston for the funeral and Irv's partner, Mr. Klein—you remember Leibowitz and Klein Industrial Uniforms? Mr. Klein comes up to me and wants to know if I intend to sell my share and I say, "What share?" Then Irv's first wife and three kids want to know what kind of gentile harpy I am for beating them out of their inheritance, and by this time I'm getting hot. So I get home and call that lawyer of Irv's and he tells me I got everything—from the condo in San Juan to half of Leibowitz and Klein to the matching burial plots in Laurel Land. Honey, I'm peeing pearls by now and I'm thinking, "Hell with 'em, it's my money, Irv left it to me and if they don't like it—screw 'em."

(*Beat.*)

For whatever reasons, they didn't seem to share in my newfound happiness. They're suing me, I'm suing them. Their lawyer's suing my lawyer, my lawyer's suing theirs. Mr. Klein's suing Mitzi Gaynor, the first Mrs. Leibowitz is suing Mr. Klein, the kids are suing their mom for divorcing their father—and the jury's in recess for the next two years trying to figure it all out.

(*Beat.*)

And that, you sweet man, is why I had to get out of Houston for a while.

[Available at New Dramatists]

DEAR JOHN
by Steve Somkin

Rena, a young woman, is seated at a table writing to her ex-lover, John. A small pile of crumpled letters is on the floor by her feet. She crumples the letter she is working on and throws it on the pile. She takes a portable tape recorder from a drawer and starts it.

RENA (*Into microphone*): Dear John. Of course I know, Edward, that your name is not John, but this is a Dear John letter. I never want to see you again—I guess you got that message when I threw your clothes into the hall—but I must tell you something. It's somewhat embarrassing . . . I hope it's as unpleasant for you as it was for me. We two knew how to share pain, didn't we, my darling? Let's do it one last time.

(RENA *stops the machine for a moment and then restarts it.*)

I am composing this letter talking into a tape recorder. I cannot put my words directly onto paper; on paper they look like translations from a foreign language, grammatical exercises, contrived and stupid and without feeling. I do wish I were looking into your eyes, or whispering in your ear, holding you close to me in our bed . . . but I never want to see you again.

Edward, John, rather, remember how we itched and scratched during the last week together? Remember you said, "People who bitch together itch together?" It was crabs. My doctor caught one of the little things and gave me a special medicated shampoo to get rid of them. You must get treated too. If you don't, God knows how many women will scratch away at their crotches . . . needlessly. I don't resent your wanting other women; that's natural, I suppose . . . crabs. Cancer the Crab. Our relationship was like a malignant cancer . . . When I'm lonely . . . What a stupid, stupid letter. He's over. He's finished.

(RENA *has stopped the machine and now restarts it.*)

Dear Edward, comma. I am writing to inform you that in all probability you have a minor venereal infection called crab lice, full stop. This is easily treated with a medication you can get from your doctor or an emergency room, full stop. It is advisable that you inform anyone with whom you have had sexual contact of the same, full stop. In all probability, Eileen is also infected, Full stop. Eileen . . . !

Dear Shithead, Eileen and her erotic acrobatics is the perfect solution to your adolescent yearnings. I'm ashamed I tolerated you for so long. By the way, you have a serious venereal disease that, unless treated, will render you impotent for life. It's probably too late already, but with immediate medical attention . . . (RENA *is fighting her tears.*) I would telephone to tell you, but I can't bear the sound of your voice.

(RENA *slams off the machine.*)

What's the matter with me? It's over. It's over. It's over.

(*Slowly and deliberately she starts the machine.*)

Dear Edward, I wonder, are there any emotions in my life that I will not first have tasted while living with you? Trying to forget you is like trying to deny my heart a place in my head. I regret that the end was so ugly. Perhaps it was the only way; perhaps at a distance, the good times will seem better for the contrast. Edward, you radiate success. I now know I need a man for whom I'm not merely an accompanist. I think that says it. Sincerely yours, Rena. P.S. Check with your doctor about the itching, it's not serious.

(RENA *heaves a sigh of relief and blows her nose.*)

Good-bye, Eddie.

[Available at New Dramatists]

RENASCENCE
by Terri Wagener

In a small town in the south, the widow Maggie Goodner is trying to raise two teenage daughters single-handedly —Edna St. Vincent, a large, unattractive mute, and Louisa May, a pretty naive sixteen-year-old who believes every man hung the moon. One day brings the arrival of Uncle Daniel, the black-sheep brother of Maggie's dead husband. Daniel spouts poetry, believes in dreams, and charms all the women in the house— while uncovering all their secrets and holding close to his own. This is Louisa May's first time alone with Daniel.

Listen, Can I Tell You Something?

LOUISA (*Tosses her head, looks around, then leans toward him*): Listen. Can I tell you something that happened to me today? And will you not tell anyone?

Well. The strangest thing happened to me today.

Today—I don't know what to do. I didn't know what to do. I still don't. (*Pause.*) Dennis took me up to his room. (*Pause.*)) I mean, he lives over the garage at his parents' house. By himself. With a private entrance and his own bathroom and everything. He took me there this afternoon after we watched the marching band practice at the football stadium. (*Pause.*) To see his newspaper clippings.

And . . . I was in his room! I mean, we walked in and he kicked these . . . underwear under the bed and then he went over and got a Kleenex to blow his nose just like he probably always does when I'm not there.

And there were these weights—like weight-lifting weights—there. And a calendar . . . and shoes.

And then he sat down! He tossed a pair of pants from the chair to the bed and then he sat down! A pair of pants!

And then. I had to go to the bathroom. And I went to the bathroom. And I went in and there was a razor by the sink. With a blade in it and everything. I checked. And there was a washcloth still damp. And a towel over the shower—with the middle dark and wrinkled, like he dried off with it sometime. And then I turned around . . . I turned around . . . and the sitdown part of the toilet was up!

(*Pause.*)

I asked him to take me home. Right then. Right away. So he did.

I think I hurt his feelings, though. But I couldn't

help it. I was scared. I mean, all jumpy inside. I can't describe it.

Am I a terrible person? Was it terrible of me to ask to go home? What do you think?

[Available at New Dramatists]

CLEVELAND
by Mac Wellman

This monologue is from the fourth scene of Mac Wellman's one-act play CLEVELAND. Joan, the daughter, has been disturbed by her Mother's strange behavior, and is trying to do the right thing in getting her mother to talk about her father's demise. Alas, the explanation explains nothing.

MOTHER: Well. All right. We were in New York
for the party congress. We had
just met the mayor of Cleveland.
Of course, *he* wasn't a Trotskyite.
He was far too fashionable for that.
A fine, big man he was, with a
fine, big, round head. He said
to your father: "Fine work, that
report on solid waste." Then he
introduced himself to me. It was
an awkward moment because, of
course, your father had no idea
what the mayor was talking about.
It seems he was at the wrong hotel.
"We're Trotskyites," we said. "My

apologies," he said. "May I buy you
a drink?" And he did. One of those
elegant little sidewalk cafes. Lovely.
   (*A sad moment.*)
We were sitting on the sidewalk, or
rather, at a table on the sidewalk. And
your father leaned over to make a point
and spilled his espresso. As he moved
forward with the saucer in his other
hand, the heel snapped off his shoe and,
well, he slid back into the chair. Of
course, the coffee got over everyone.
And the chair leg broke and—it was
quite remarkable—he did a nice
little, wholly unintentional back-
flip into the street. I shall never
forget the sight of his shoes—the
soles of them—as they lifted high
into the air. He was trying to save
the cup, poor dear. But it shattered
in the street, and then the first car
ran over it. And the saucer, which had
been undamaged, miraculously, up to that
point. He was quite a fastidious man.
The second car ran over your father.
Quite a large car. A limo, I think.
"My word!" said the mayor. What a
strange thing to say. Of course, he was
dead. Your father, I mean. That's about it.
Coffee?

[Available at New Dramatists]

FENCES
by August Wilson

Rose's devotion to her husband, Troy, stems from her recognition of the possibilities of her life without him: a succession of abusive men, their babies, a life of partying and running the streets; the church; or aloneness with its attendant pain and frustrations. Troy, however, has just told Rose that he has been seeing another woman because she makes him feel like a new man, like he hasn't been "standing in the same place for seventeen years." The following monologue is her response to his complaints of dissatisfaction with his life.

ROSE: I been standing with you! I been right here with you, Troy. I got a life too. I gave seventeen years of my life to stand in the same spot with you. Don't you think I ever wanted other things? Don't you think I had dreams and hopes? What about my life? What about me, Troy. Don't you think it ever crossed my mind to want to know other men? That I wanted to lay up somewhere and forget about my responsibilities? That I wanted someone to make me laugh so I could feel good. You not the only one who's got wants and needs. But I held onto you, Troy. I took all my feelings, my wants and needs, my dreams . . . and I buried them inside you. I planted a seed and watched and prayed over it. I planted myself inside you and waited to bloom. And it didn't take me no seventeen years to find out the soil was hard and rocky and it wasn't never gonna bloom. But I held onto you, Troy. I held you tighter. You was my husband. I owed you everything I had. Every part of me I could find to give you. And upstairs in that room . . . with the darkness falling in on me . . . I gave everything I had to try and erase the doubt that you wasn't the finest man in the world. And wherever you was going . . . I wanted to be there with you! 'Cause you was my husband. 'Cause that's the only way I was gonna survive as your wife. You always talking about what you give and what you don't have to give. But you take too Troy. You take . . . and don't even know nobody's giving.

[Published by New American Library]

MA RAINEY'S BLACK BOTTOM
by August Wilson

In the middle of their recording session, one of the musicians happens to mention that the song Ma Rainey is recording has also been done by Bessie Smith. Ma protests that she was the first, that she taught Bessie, that everyone is imitating her. Ma Rainey's manner is simple and direct: She's been in the business longer than anybody and she knows the score.

MA RAINEY: I been doing this a long time. Ever since I was a little girl. I don't care what nobody else do. That's what gets me so mad with Irvin. White folks try to be put out with you all the time. Too cheap to buy me a Coca-Cola. I lets them know it, though. Ma don't stand for no shit. Wanna take my voice and trap it in them fancy boxes with all them buttons and dials . . . and then too cheap to buy me a Coca-Cola. And it don't cost but a nickel a bottle.

They don't care nothing about me. All they want is my voice. Well, I done learned that, and they gonna treat me like I want to be treated no matter how much it hurt them. They back there now calling me all kinds of names . . . calling me everything but a child of

God. But they can't do nothing else. They ain't got what they wanted yet. As soon as they get my voice down on them recording machines, then it's just like if I'd be some whore and they roll over and put their pants on. Ain't got no use for me then. I know what I'm talking about. You watch. Irvin right there with the rest of them. He don't care nothing about me either. He's been my manager for six years, always talking about sticking together, and the only time he had me in his house was to sing for some of his friends.

If you colored and can make them some money, then you all right with them. Otherwise, you just a dog in the alley. I done made this company more money from my records than all the other recording artists they got put together. And they wanna balk about how much this session is costing them.

[Published by New American Library]

Monologues
for
Men

I NEVER SANG FOR MY FATHER
by Robert Anderson

Gene, a forty-year-old widower, is the ideal son: obedient, loyal, eager to please, always there when his parents need him. He loved his recently deceased mother very much, and has tried to remain close to his father. Gene is in love with a woman in California, and wants to move there and marry her. He invited his father to come live with him in California, but his father rejected the offer and accused him of not caring.

GENE: That night I left my father's house forever . . . I took the first right and the second left . . and this time I went as far as California.

Peggy and I visited him once or twice . . . and then he came to California to visit us, and had a fever and swollen ankles, and we put him in a hospital, and he never left . . . The reason we gave, and which he could accept, for not leaving . . . the swollen ankles. But the real reason . . . the arteries were hardening, and he gradually over several years slipped into complete and speechless senility . . . with his life centered in his burning eyes.

When I would visit him, and we would sit and look

at each other, his eyes would mist over and his nostrils would pinch with emotion . . . But I never could learn what the emotion was . . . anger . . . or love . . . or regret . . .

One day, sitting in his wheelchair and staring without comprehension at television . . . he died . . . alone . . . without even an orange in his hand.

Death ends life . . . but it does not end a relationship, which struggles on in the survivor's mind . . . toward some resolution, which it never finds.

Peggy said I would not accept the sadness of the world . . . What did it matter if I never loved him, or if he never loved me? . . . Perhaps she was right . . . But, still, when I hear the word Father . . .

(GENE *cannot express it. There is still the longing, the emotion. He looks around—out—as though he would finally be able to express it, but he can only say:*)

It matters.

(GENE *turns and walks slowly away.*)

[Published by Dramatists Play Service]

THE LOCKED ROOM
by Arthur Carter

Captain Luther is a black medical officer assigned to temporary duty to the 1066th General Hospital in Le Havre during World War II. He is accused by a white nurse of having attempted to rape her. He has withheld information from the investigating officer to protect the nurse—information that would prove his innocence. In the speech that follows he has finally decided to tell the truth to Major Beckman, the executive officer in the hospital.

LUTHER: Major, please, let me talk. I'm going to tell you the truth now, Major, the whole truth and nothing but the truth, so help me God. You're right to be angry with me, Major, because it's true, I haven't been telling you the whole truth. I told you as much of the truth as I felt I could. I just couldn't come out with the whole truth—you'll understand, I think, when I tell you why. My temporary duty here was some kind of a mistake, I know—I was the first black officer to serve with the hospital and I felt very uncomfortable being here. Maggie Collins was the first one to try to make me feel I was welcome, a part of the hospital.

We became friends, working on the same ward together, and then slowly we started to become something more than friends. We kept it from everyone
else in the hospital, but we fell in love with each other,
Major. And then that night at the club we both had a
few drinks—I suppose that gave us the extra courage
we needed—and we decided to get together, to be
alone, really alone, for the first time. She left the
dancing, telling people she was feeling dizzy, and I
followed her outside. We agreed on the story we'd tell
if we got caught together and we both stuck to that
part of the story. But what we both said happened in
the Locked Room "B"—neither Maggie's nor my story
is true. This is the hard part to get out, Major. It's
going to be hard for me to find the words. I feel very
ashamed telling it. Not because it was shameful! No,
it's not that! It's the telling of it—the putting it into
words. We were in love. We were alone, really, for
the first time. I was so excited I was shaking all over. I
couldn't stop. I had never been alone with a white
woman before. I was shaking so I couldn't even unbut-
ton . . . I don't know why I tried, nothing was happening inside. I felt so embarrassed . . . But Maggie said,
"Please, Luther, there's no reason to feel embarrassed.
Let me help, Luther, make something happen." She
unbuttoned my fly and took me into her mouth . . .
"Oh my God, Maggie, you're beautiful—just beautiful!" I said. And just at that moment, the lights came
on, a figure stood in the doorway and we heard him
say, "I'm Jesus Christ come back to punish all sinners
for their evil ways!" The next moment the lights were
snapped off and the figure in the doorway disappeared.
I said, "Oh my God, Maggie . . ." and I tried to

embrace her. But she pushed me away and screamed, "Don't—don't touch me!" And she ran out. What Maggie did was so sweet, so wonderful, so loving—I was so moved, Major, so touched, I started to cry. It was at that wonderful loving moment that it happened. I tried to see her the next day, but she avoided me. When I finally got to speak to her, she attacked me, threatened me—the shock she'd had turned her against me, changed everything between us. The rest you know, Major.

[Available at New Dramatists]

THE TROUBLE WITH EUROPE
by Paul D'Andrea

Inspector Jogot (rhymes with "Godot") is in his late twenties or early thirties. Handsome, vain, arrogant, intellectual, lonely, he is the greatest criminal detective in France. He makes up for his abandonment as a child by relentlessly finding guilt in everyone he meets and punishing it. In the first monologue he is sitting in a jetliner trying to arrest Tilbury, a charismatic, violence-prone American ex-cowboy who is actually on the same mission as Jogot, to find out what is wrong with the modern era and remedy it in six days. Tilbury's native charm brings out the endearing and affectionate side of Jogot's nature.

JOGOT: Why did she do that? To you? I mean, just up and kiss you like that? Out of nowhere?
(*Beat.*)
I have a birthmark over my right shoulder blade. Some say it enhances my male beauty. All I know is, I have quite a bit of trouble with women bothering me. Big, good-looking women. It's been this way ever since I had hair on my upper lip. Last spring I was

carrying a wand of pussy willows through a giant airport. Would you believe how the women peeked at me! Just before boarding, one of them said she couldn't resist, reached out and touched the pussy willows! Do you know what I said? I said, "Please. I know. Believe me, I know how it is. But please . . . don't touch my pussy willows." She just stopped bothering my pussy willows and *peeked* a little.

Ah, guilty. Everyone's guilty. I like guilt. I dislike children, I loathe Europe, and I particularly hate Paris. I would like nothing better than to get her entire population behind bars.

I am an intellectual. I started as a butcher's boy. One day, near the university, I was trying to get my tie out of my bicycle chain. I opened the wrong door, looking for help—carrying my bicycle like this—and wandered by accident into a lecture hall. Four years later I emerged the greatest intellect of the West. I know what I want. I despise beauty, the moon, and the milkweed sail. I love hunting men. And women too. They're very guilty too. Uh, do women usually go around kissing you?

Wandering into that lecture hall was an accident and meeting you was an accident. I'm enjoying this.

In the second Monologue, Tilbury speaks as he and Jogot are walking, lost, deep underground through a limestone tunnel they've fallen into in their search for the trouble with Europe. What drives him is his vision of this woman he once knew, Tuli Latum.

TILBURY: The darker it gets down here, the more I seem to see Tuli. Right now, in my mind's eye, I can see her blasting across the American highway in the luminous pre-dawn purple, her long legs astride a thousand chromium horsepower.

(*He pauses, putting one boot up on a rock.*)

Y'see, I've known Tuli since she first started filling out her jeans. Did I, uh, ever happen to describe to you her breasts?

Don't get me wrong now. She's a chaste and modest girl. But active. She's almost always in motion—swinging that long leg like a lasso up over a horse, or swishing three hundred and sixty degrees of horizon up into her bright hair, or getting down under the semi to check on a brake line. You kind of get a glimpse now and then—blouses being what they are—even if you're not trying to, even if she's not trying to—even if no one's trying to, blouses are what they are and breasts are what they are and where they are. And willy-nilly, life being what it is, you get a glimpse now and then—of other worlds.

Close your eyes, Jogot, and imagine to yourself milk . . . Not a vessel of milk, but milk itself. Have you got the milk in your mind? Now imagine its perfect and spatially limitless globeness folding back on itself. Twice. Have you got that? Twice. Now picture the delicate film that covers milk when you heat it ever so carefully. Can you see it? That delicate film? Now imagine that weight previously envisioned, supported, and contained only by that delicate film-skin, almost bursting, suspended, but not quite bursting—all held in on itself by that delicate film.

If you were to touch it—it would burst immensely!

[Published by Samuel French]

THE DOWNSIDE
by Richard Dresser

Jeff is a skilled player in corporate politics. He has an outwardly successful life, with apparently everything he could want. But he hungers for more. He has just fired Ben, his best friend, in order to preserve his own position in the corporation. Now he is seated at the conference table, alone except for a speaker box, where Dave, the head of the corporation, is listening. Jeff is suddenly wracked by doubts about his life. He is isolated from everyone else in the department, and desperate to make some kind of connection. The speaker box is his last hope. Dave has just assured him that his job is safe. This is his response.

JEFF: I hate to fire Ben. We were friends a long time . . . we used to get together socially quite a bit, but that kind of tapered off . . he started to have problems in his marriage. The last time I was at his house was last spring. My wife was still in the hospital, it was right after my daughter was born. Ben invited me over for dinner and the three of us sat out back of his house eating and drinking and Ben was drinking a whole lot that night and I remember I started getting these vibes from his wife, you know? Her knee brushes against me and maybe it's an accident, maybe not. Well, we sat there a whole long time, till it started to get dark and Ben went inside. I thought he was just getting another drink, but he didn't come back. I sit there talking to his wife and I can hardly see her, but I'm getting this feeling from her so I figure, well, what the hell, we've had a few drinks, we're all friends, what's a little kiss? But it was one of those situations that just got out of control. I mean, one minute we're discussing the crabgrass and the next minute we're rolling around in it right next to the barbecue, and everything was in darkness and—Dave, you have to understand, I did not force myself on this woman . . . it was like something rose up out of the ground and pulled us together because we couldn't stop. I bet you've been in situations like that.

(*Beat.*)

Afterwards, we lie on the grass and the house is dark except for a light in one window upstairs, and as I'm staring at the house the light goes out. I didn't know what to do. She starts putting on her clothes, very casually, humming to herself, then she piles up the dirty dishes and goes into the kitchen, like nothing had happened. The kitchen light goes on and I see her at the sink washing the dishes. So I get dressed and start toward the house, I figure, Ben is my friend, I'm going to look him in the eye, because this whole thing was more like a car accident than seduction, but just when I'm about to open the screen door I stop—something stops me cold—and I walk around and get in my car. And I drive to the hospital to see my wife and baby daughter.

(*Beat.*)

It was fear, Dave. I didn't have the courage to face him. And he knew, I'm convinced he knew what happened. Neither one of us ever mentioned it, but he knew. I've never told anyone this. I have no one to talk to . . . I would like to be able to talk to someone.

(*Beat.*)

I would like to have the courage to do right.

[Available at New Dramatists]

WAR STORY
by Gus Edwards

This monologue deals with the frustrations of being poor and not being part of polite society. The piece is from an unproduced work entitled MOODY'S CAFE. Moody's cafe is a place where the down-and-out, the disenfranchised gather to interrelate.

WILSON: I never go to the movies. And I'll tell you why. Movies are a waste of time. They never show you about life. Always some goddamn lie. That's all they're good for. Telling lies . . . Last picture I seen was a war picture. That was some years ago. Never was any war like that. That was just a load of bullshit. Bunch of boys running around with rifles and shouting out and shooting. War wasn't like that. I was in the war, Second World War, I know.

Let me tell you a story about the Second World War, see if you ever see anything like that in the movies.

I was in the infantry. All the colored boys anybody knew was in the infantry. One day when the Army made their roundup, they was taking everybody in sight. Didn't care who. Long as you was young and strong, they took you in . . .

Now, at that time on the block, there was a sissy boy named Vance. Everybody know'd all about him. Vance didn't try to keep nothing secret. He used to walk all over Harlem with his ass high and rolling, talking in this voice like he was some kind of woman. Now, if there was a person you'd guess the Army would refuse, this fellow Vance woulda been the one. But you would be guessing wrong. They took him in just like everybody else. Put him through basic training and sent him overseas.

Now, I didn't see that sissy boy all through the war years. Didn't even think about him, for that matter. Then one day when it was all over, and we was all mustered out, I was walking down the street here in Harlem and who do I see, walking proud, looking healthy and still wearing his Army uniform. Good old Vance. But on his chest was all kinds of ribbons and medals and I don't know what else.

"Goddamn, Vance," I said to him, "look like you went on to be some kind of hero."

"Baby," he answered back, still talking in that high, woman voice, "Mother was a sergeant in charge of her little chickadees. One day the German Army surrounded Mother's chicks and had them trapped so bad they couldn't get out. Well, when Mother heard this, she couldn't let that be. Some a them little goslings were part of Mama's special flock. If you know what I mean. So I took a submachine gun and went in for my birds. All of them . . . And in the process I had to shoot me a whole lot of German soldiers. But God was with me and I succeeded in my mission. And when I come out, all my little birds was with me . . . All the other men and officers looked at me like I was some kind of miracle. They started shouting and clapping. And saying that I should get some kind of medal. And they didn't just give me one. They gave me a whole bunch . . . But what I did wasn't nothing special. Just a mother hen protecting her little chicks."

Now tell me, you ever see anything like that in the movies? Just lies. And more lies. That's all they ever show up on that screen.

[Available at New Dramatists]

LIVING AT HOME
by Anthony Giardina

John is a twenty-year-old college dropout and the son of Eddie Bogle, owner of Riverside Bowling Alley in Watertown, Massachusetts. His brother David plans to attend medical school and his sister Miggsy was just accepted to Barnard; both have bright futures ahead of them. Meanwhile, John, bewildered and dissatisfied, sits home and watches news coverage of the Kennedy assassination. After David announces he's getting married, John explains why he dropped out of college.

JOHN: You want to know why I left? Okay, you got it.

One night last January, I'm sitting in this bar in Amherst, talking to some girl. I started telling her this story. When my brother and I were little, we used to play this game: Robert the Robot. One of us had to be Robert the Robot, and Robert, see, Robert had to climb down the steps leading to the basement and catch the other one. You had to walk like a robot. You had to be—very mechanical. Mostly I had to be Robert because David was better at hiding. So I'd hunch my shoulders up and climb down the stairs, chasing David. Only he was nowhere to be found. I'd do my mechanical walk pretending to look for him, but, see, I had no idea. And pretty soon I'd scare myself. Being Robert the Robot, having to go through the motions, scared me. So I'd sit down, I'd stop being Robert, and David would come out all pissed off and say "What's the matter?" The only thing I could ever say was, "I don't like being Robert. I don't want to be Robert anymore."

A hush falls over the bar. I realize everybody's been listening. I looked around, saw all these college heads nodding sagely at the profoundness of my Robert story, and had a revelation. I realized that in all this time, I hadn't succeeded in shaking myself free of this family, but only tied myself tighter, that my friends were not gods, not the golden generation that was going to change the world, but simply the sons of the lower middle class, playing at getting an education, that we would take our lower-middle-class attitudes with us wherever we went because you can't shake loose of them, you can't just say, "I don't want to be Robert anymore" and make it work. You've got your roots in a bowling alley and in the streets of some town like Watertown. You are Eddie Bogle's son, and you carry him inside you, and try as you might to suppress that part to be something else, sooner or later you find yourself in a bar telling a story you thought happened in another life, and suddenly the jig is up. You can't fool yourself any longer.

[Published by Dramatists Play Service]

THE CHILD
by Anthony Giardina

Thomas, twenty-seven, an idealistic man who drives a milk truck, and his wife Leah, twenty-three, a first-year medical student, struggle to decide whether to have the baby which is growing inside of Leah or to abort it. They finally decide to have an abortion, mainly on Thomas's insistence. In this monologue, Thomas discusses a recurring dream of his in which he meets the child that they were going to name Tonio.

THOMAS: I keep having this dream.
Can I tell you this dream?
I know you must not like me much just now, but can I tell you this dream I keep having?
(*Beat.*)
We have a little boy. Leah.
You're not in it.
Just me and this boy. In my dream he looks like a little Indian.
So wild I don't know where he comes from.
We're up in the mountains, hiking, I guess.
We see this bird.

And the boy, Tonio, can't get over this bird, cannot take his eyes off it.

So I sit down on a rock to get out this book I have. This bird book, *Birds of North America*. I want to find this bird so I can explain everything to Tonio. His markings, his mating habits, where he lives.

When I find it, I look up to tell him.

He's far away from me.

On the edge of the mountain.

Making like a bird.

Flapping his arms.

Then he jumps.

I watch him jump, it's too quick for me to say anything.

I sit there with an open book, but I'm not afraid.

Because I expect to see him any minute.

Flying above me.

With the markings and the mating habits of a thing I have to look up in books to find out about.

So I sit on this rock. Waiting.

And finally he flies up. Like I knew he would.

And I smile to see him, Tonio, in the trees, branch to branch.

Tonio over the mountain.

Then he swoops down over me.

He says, "Come on, Dad. Jump. It's fun."

(*Beat.*)

So I go to the edge.

I stand there.

I can see right down to the bottom.

I'm holding a bird book.

I know everything there is to know about birds from the book.

I know I'm not a bird.

I feel so scared.
I look up.
He's gone.
(*Beat.*)
No. Christ. No.
I want you.
I want you.
I want you. Please don't leave me here, Tonio. Come
back. I'll jump. I swear. Just come back. You'll see
me arms spread, legs out, one golden image of your
father I'll give you—
(*Beat.*)
Tonio.
Forgive me. Forgive me. Forgive me.

[Available at New Dramatists]

THE BRIXTON RECOVERY
by Jack Gilhooley

Mickey is an Irish-American light-heavyweight boxer who has faded from prominence. He has become a member of the small but vivid Yankee journeyman fighters who are playing out the string in Europe and Latin America. More often than not, they are willing to take a dive for one more paycheck. He has moved in with Shirley, a pretty and bright West Indian bar-maid living in the Brixton section of London. Despite his long pugilistic career, Mickey's faculties are still intact and one of the things that appeals to Shirley is Mickey's story-telling sense.

MICKEY: Ya ever been t'Mexico? Ya think Brixton stinks, ya oughta try Mexico. You're livin' in the lap of luxury, here. I fought Mexico once. Small arena outside Guadalajara. Christ, what a gig that was. I decided t'check the ring before they opened the house 'cause I'd heard that they spray the outsider's corner with this solution that makes ya drowsy. I walk inta the house an' there's this huge cyclone fence risin' up behind the fifth row. It goes all the way around an' it reaches t'the ceilin'. So I sez t'myself, "Shit, if this ain't the last straw. Now they got me fightin' in a cage, fer chrissakes." Well, I decide t'hell with it, I'll take it out onna greaser. So my bout comes up and I come inta the ring. Now ya gotta understand that when I fight, I'm blind t'anything but my opponent on accounta the lights and on accounta my concentration. Everythin' else is a blank. Well, I coldcock the guy with a left-right-left inna third an' I head fer the showers and fer the promoters 'cause those guys are notorious for skippin' with the purse. Afterwards, I decide t'take in the main event 'cause they're also light-heavies an' one never knows when one's paths might cross. Well, I walk into the house and the first five rows are occupied by gringos an' the Mexican racketeers in silk suits and expensive jewelry, including a hooker hangin' offa each arm. On the other side of the fence are the peasants and they're drunk an' screamin' curses at the rich people as well as the fighters. There's fights breakin' out all over the place an' a couple of them have just killed a chicken that's still quiverin' an' they're bustin' up the seats t'make a fire. An' one guy's laying in a pool of his own puke an' another guy's bleedin' from a knife wound in his face only he's too drunk t'move. An' there's this one guy onna top row where it's real dark, but not quite dark enough so that you can faintly see that he's got this dame doin' t'him what I will leave to the imagination, seein' that I'm in mixed company. An' every time their boy scores big, the peasants leap up on this cyclone fence an' shake back an' forth till I think the whole fuckin' arena's gonna collapse on my head. I'll never forget that sight. Not just men—women and children too—rockin' back an' forth on that fence screamin' bloody murder. Then all of a sudden, one of them spits inta the first five rows, an' the cops—who up to this time were loungin' around enjoyin' the fight—they go bananas. They storm the area, swingin' their clubs at anyone they can reach till they get the one they think done it and they proceed t'bash that poor son of a bitch half t'death. Then, as fast as it started, it's over. The cops split an' go back t'loungin' around an' watchin' the fight an' they leave the people there t'bleed all over each other. An' it's not until then that I realize—as I'm lookin' at this spectacle that coulda got a standing ovation in hell— it's not until then that I realize that I wasn't the one inna cage. No sirree, not me.

[Published by Samuel French]

YANKEE DAWG YOU DIE
by *Philip Kan Gotanda*

Bradley Yamashita is an Asian-American actor in his mid-to-late twenties who very much wants to make it in Hollywood. He has a strong political conscience.

The First Japanese Rock 'n' Roll Star

It was night. It was one of those typical summer nights in the Valley. The hot, dry heat of the day was gone. Just the night air filled with swarming mosquitoes, the sound of those irrigation pumps sloshing away. And that peculiar smell that comes from those empty fruit crates stacked in the sheds with their bits and pieces of smashed apricot still clinging to the sides and bottoms. They've been sitting in the packing sheds all day long. And by evening they fill the night air with the unmistakable pungent odor of sour and sweet that only a summer night, a summer night in the San Joaquin Valley can give you.

And that night, as with every night, I was lost. And that night, as with every night of my life, I was looking for somewhere, some place that belonged to me.

I took my Dad's car 'cause I just had to go for a drive. "Where you going, son? We got more work to do in the sheds separating out the fruit." "Sorry Dad." . . .

I'd drive out to the Yonemoto's and pick up my girl, Bess. Her mother'd say, "Drive carefully and take good care of my daughter—she's Pa and me's only girl." "Sure, Mrs. Yonemoto" . . .

And I'd drive. Long into the night. Windows down, my girl Bess beside me, the radio blasting away . . . . But it continued to escape me—this thing, place, that belonged to me.

And then the deejay came on the radio, "Here's a new record by a hot new artist, 'Carol,' by Neil Sedaka!" Neil who? Sedaka? Did you say, "Sedaka"? (*Pronunciation gradually becomes Japanese.*) Sedaka. Sedaka. Sedaka. Sedaakaa. As in my father's cousin's brother-in-law's name, Hiroshi Sedaka? What's that you say? The first Japanese American rock'n'roll star! What's that? (*Disbelief.*) Nooo. His parents raise strawberries down in Oxnard?

Neil Sedaka. That name. I couldn't believe it. Suddenly everything was all right. I was there. Driving in my car, windows down, girl beside me—and that radio blasting away with a goddamned Buddahead singing on the radio . . . Neil Sedaka!

I knew. I just knew for once, wherever I drove to that night, the road belonged to me.

[Available at New Dramatists]

HOW I GOT THAT STORY
by Amlin Gray

The setting is a war-torn Asian city. The Reporter has arrived there what seems to him like years before. His first intention was to stay absolutely objective, outside of what he saw, but a deepening fascination led him to try to become a "member" of the struggling, suffering country. As had objectivity, this approach failed him. He is now a helpless vagrant. At the beginning of the play, the then-cub gave the audience an eager running commentary on his experiences. Later he lost touch with them. Now he notices them once again.

REPORTER: Hello. You look familiar. I believe I used to talk to you. Are you my readers?

I'm doing very well. Last night I found a refrigerator carton that would shelter a whole family with their pigs and chickens. Next to it a trash pile I can live off for a week. If I can find my way back. I kind of get lost on these streets sometimes.

Sometimes I can stand like this and drift in all directions through the city, soaking up the sounds.

(REPORTER *sits down on the pavement.*)

There's a firefight out there beyond the border of

the city. Tracers from a helicopter gunship, see, they're streaming down like water from a hose. Green tracers coming up to meet them now, they climb up toward the ship and then they drop and their green fire goes out. They fall and hit some tree somewhere. The lumber industry is almost dead in Am-bo Land. A fact I read. The trees are all so full of metal that the lumber mills just break their saw blades.

Magnesium flares. They're floating down on little parachutes. I floated down like that once. Everything is turning silver and the shadows are growing and growing. The street looks like the surface of the moon.

[Published by Dramatists Play Service. Also available in the anthology *Coming of Age: American Plays and the Vietnam War*, published by Theatre Communications Group.]

THE FANTOD
by Amlin Gray

The setting is a secluded English manor house at the time of the Crimean War. The speaker is Sir Tristam Northmoor. As his title indicates, he is of noble birth, but many years spent in the East have involved him in experiments with mind-expanding "fantods" of an intensely un-English character. Having invaded the Marryat household, Sir Tristam has made exotic advances to the very young and sheltered Rachel Marryat. This is the last of them.

SIR TRISTAM: Both of us are sitting. We are sitting both together in the Pavilion Room. Ahhhh . . .

(SIR TRISTAM *sings the room tone.*)

Do you feel us both together in the same enclosure? Oooo . . . That is the tone of my Being. Do you hear it? Oooo . . . And this is your tone. They are both the same. Oooo . . .

Now close your eyes. You are now to think of the dress you are wearing. Every ruffle. Every twist of thread. From the hem and up, all circles, each one smaller than the last, and now the waist, the smallest, and move up and up . . . Don't cheat me. I can feel every thought. So rare these thoughts the very air they cross seems gross.

Now think of the garment underneath your dress. Yes. Every stitch. A camisole. It runs along, a swelling here, a valley there, a dark place. Now the garment under that. It's made of silk. It's smooth and cool against your skin. Now think of your skin. The nerves that reach out to the surface reach back deep inside you, all the way to touch your deepest Being.

(SIR TRISTAM *stays where he is; he doesn't literally touch her.*)

Feel my hand. It doesn't touch your skin. It touches *you*. It touches me inside you. I am you more deeply than you've ever been yourself. Say yes.

Don't move. Stay with me. We two stand alone, outside the moral laws. No, I can see you stiffen. Here. Take this.

(SIR TRISTAM *takes a small white cube of opium out of his pocket.*)

This is madjoon. Pure. We're not bound any longer. Spirit and Life. Pure Being. Eat.

Why be afraid? We're both of us beyond the pale. Take it.

(SIR TRISTAM *reaches again into his pocket.*)

Do you see? I have as much as we can ever want. I usually take one cube.

(*Scornfully.*)

One cube. In time past I would count. But you and I are past the realm of numbers. I can take this much. And this much.

(SIR TRISTAM *gobbles both handfuls.*)

Do you feel it, Rachel? You and I are free. We're streaming up into the sky so fast the wind blows God's hair. There He is below us now. He's staring at us. Do you see His face? He looks like a child who's been punished and He doesn't understand. He's lost His Kingdom. A new Creation has made Him a thing of the past. I'm the new Creator! My Creation is Sir Tristam Northmoor, engendered on Myself and by Myself! Come with me, Rachel! Come with me!

[Published by Dramatists Play Service]

LANDSCAPE OF THE BODY
by John Guare

Raulito is an attractive, sexually intimidating Latin man (he wears a gold lamé evening gown over his business suit, has a pompadour, and wears diamond rings). He makes his living by conniving newlyweds into paying for honeymoon trips which they never take. He slept with Betty's sister Rosalie, and now expects to seduce Betty.

RAULITO (*talking to* BETTY): That is exactly what your sister Rosalie said to me the first time we met. We would curl up on her pullout sleep sofa, now *your* pullout sleep sofa, and I would tell her my dream, to one night turn on the TV and hear the *Late Show* say "And tonight our guest is *me!*"

Thank you, Johnny. I'm from Cuba. We lived on the other side of the island. From Havana.

(RAULITO *sits beside the desk as if he were the guest on the* Tonight Show *and* BETTY *were the host.*)

Poor. You never saw such poor. We were so poor *that*. You know those jokes? He was so fat *that*. She was so dumb *that*. Well, we were so *poor* that. When I was wearing rags, I was running around naked. This part of Cuba that we called country, I think any normal thinking person would call it the jungle. Occasionally, a magazine would appear in our village and I'd see the pictures of evening gowns and spangles and barrettes in the hair and these high heels. I didn't know till later that was what women wore. I thought that was rich people. I thought if you were rich and lived in the city or lived in America that was what the average American family hung around in. The Revolution came. I saw Che Guevera this close. We left Cuba. We got to Florida. Where I found out that those uniforms with diamonds and lace did not belong to the typical American man. But a few years ago, I was shopping in the Salvation Army for a winter coat and I came upon this real Rita Hayworth special. A beautiful 1940s evening gown for twenty-five cents. I bought it. Why not. The dreams we have as kids they're the dreams we never get over. I put it on over my suit. I feel rich. I feel successful.

(RAULITO *begins to spin so the dress flares out. He advances seductively on* BETTY, *now waving the dress like a matador's cape in front of her.* BETTY *is terrified. He shows her no mercy.*)

I feel I can get out of the jungle and get to America and twirl and twirl. Feeling good outside, I start to feel good inside. I start Honeymoon Holidays. I want to start a family. I want to start a life. Betty, your sister went with me. Your sister would let me dance with her first. Then she would let me sleep with her after and dreams would come out of our heads like little Turkish moons. We would salute. Betty?

[Published by Dramatists Play Service]

THE HOUSE OF BLUE LEAVES
by John Guare

Artie Shaughnessy is a forty-five-year-old, lower-middle-class man with an unstable wife, a crazy son, and a flighty mistress. After caring for his wife for six months, he decides he wants to go to Hollywood to be a popular songwriter. Despite disaster at a recent amateur-night contest, Artie is confident that his songs could be big hits. With some coaxing from his girlfriend, Bunny, he finally calls up Billy, a childhood buddy of his who is a highly successful producer in Hollywood to see if he can help Artie "get a foot in the door."

ARTIE: Billy, I'm thinking I got to get away—not just a vacation, but make a change, get a break, if you know what I'm getting at . . . Bananas is fine. She's right here. We were just thinking about you—*No, it's not fine*. Billy, this sounds cruel to say, but Bananas is as dead for me as Georgia is for you. I'm in love with a remarkable, wonderful girl—yeah, she's here too—who I should've married years ago. No, we didn't know her years ago—I only met her two months ago—yeah . . .

(ARTIE *secretively pulls the phone off to the corner.*)

It's kind of funny, a chimpanzee knocked me in the back and kinked my back out of whack, and I went to this health club to work it out and in the steam section with all the steam I got lost and I went into this steam room and there was Bunny—yeah, just towels—I mean, you could make a movie out of this, it was so romantic. She couldn't see me and she started talking about the weight she had taken off and the food she had to give up and she started talking about duckling with orange sauce and oysters baked with spinach and shrimps baked in the juice of melted sturgeon eyes which caviar comes from—well, you know me and food and I got so excited and the steam's getting thicker and thicker and I ripped off my towel and kind of raped her . . . and she was quiet for a long time and then she said one of the greatest lines of all time . . . She said, "There's a man in here." . . . And she was in her sheet like a toga and I was toga'd up and I swear, Billy, we were gods and goddesses and the steam bubbled up and swirled and it was Mount Olympus. I'm a new man, Billy—a new man—and I got to make a start before it's too late and I'm calling you, crawling on my hands and knees—no, not like that, I'm standing up straight and talking to my best buddy and saying, Can I come see you and bring Bunny and talk over old times . . . I'll pay my own way. I'm not asking you so much and I read about you in the columns and *Conduct of Life* is playing at the Museum of Modern Art next week and I get nervous calling you and that Doris Day pic—well, Bunny and I fell out of our loge seats—no, Bananas couldn't see it— she don't go out of the house much . . . I get nervous about calling you because, well, you know, and I'm not asking for any auld lang syne treatment, but it must be kind of lonely with Georgia gone and we sent five dollars in to the Damon Runyon Cancer Fund like Walter Winchell said to do and we're gonna send more and it must be kind of lonely and the three of us—Bunny and you and me—could have some laughs. What do you say? You write me and let me know your schedule and we can come any time. But soon. Okay, buddy? Okay? No, this is my call. I'm paying for this call so you don't have to worry—talking to you I get all opened up. You still drinking rye? Jack Daniels! Set out the glasses—open the bottle—no, I'll bring the bottle—we'll see you soon. Good night, Billy.

(*The call is over.*)

Soon, Billy. Soon. Soon.

(ARTIE *hangs up.*)

[Published by Viking Press]

HEY YOU, LIGHT MAN!
by Oliver Hailey

Ashley Knight, whose real name is Orville Sheden, is a handsome, middle-aged matinee idol. He has not touched his wife in years, and she has never seen him act. After twenty years of marriage, he has left her and their children. Knight reveals to a simple young woman named Lula (with whom he is fascinated) the difficulty he had being a father. He reflects on one specific incident at the circus.

KNIGHT: Once when he was a little fellow, I took him to the circus. He and I—a day together. I was trying. But you know how it is with little kids when you take them somewhere. The way they can get away from you.

Well, he'd dash this way, that way—I'd chase after him. It was a real struggle for a while. But finally he seemed to settle down—things began to go a little better. And . . . and by the end of the day I was really feeling good. He was smiling at me. I was smiling at him. You know it was a—a relationship. Why, we were even laughing as we came in the front door. But there was my wife—and I'll never forget the look on her face when she saw us. That smile—and then she said, "He's not ours. You brought home the wrong child, you fool." I was sick about it. He was such a nice little fellow.

The kid I brought home was blond and ours was dark. She said I wasn't even trying. After a while the police came, brought ours, took the other one, and fined me twenty-five dollars.

I can still see my boy sitting in that police car, his teeth clinched, glaring at me, an ice cream cone in each hand, refusing to get out. He didn't want to leave the policeman. And the other kid, he didn't want to go with the policeman. He cried and begged not to have to go away. And my wife, she kept screaming, "What kind of a father are you? Go get your own kid, damn it!"

It was an awful moment. I knew I was pulling for the wrong kid. But she screamed again—by this time there were neighbors, they began to hoot—so, I carried the other little kid to the police car, he hugged me good-bye. And then I carried my boy into the house and as we walked, he rubbed both ice cream cones in my face—and the crowd cheered. And it was then I knew. I really wasn't up to being a father. She said I was through anyway. I'd never take our kids out again. And so I came here.

[Published by Dramatists Play Service]

WHO'S HAPPY NOW?
by Oliver Hailey

It is Horse's forty-first birthday. He has succeeded in living longer than his father, who died at forty. Horse admired his father a great deal and almost looked forward to dying at age forty to honor him.

Horse resents his mother for marrying another man on the first anniversary of his father's death, and shares these feelings with his son Richard, a smart boy of fourteen, and his estranged wife, Mary.

HORSE: That's a lie. I knew why she married again! I was fourteen! And if I hadn't been old enough to figure it out, my buddy would of told me anyway. He said it to me. "She wants it again"—that's what he said. "She likes it." You think that didn't just about kill me? My own mother? She liked it? She wanted it again? She couldn't go on living without it? You see, that's the kind of mama I had, boy. And the kind of grandmama you had. What do you think of that?

Not women—no! I'm talking about *mothers*, boy! How would you feel if you found out *your* mother liked it?!

Why, I left that whore and never went back there

again—till you made me go back, Mary. All those years I just sent her them postcards. Remember me telling you about them postcards, Mary?

They were pretty funny, they were! Pretty funny! You see, my mama kept crying her real reason for marrying again was so I could go on and be a lawyer like my papa. That was supposed to be very important to her. And this second man was going to pay for it! You can believe that one, can't you? Well, I left home age fourteen, and I sent her a postcard once a month, regular. No address, just the town I was in that month, and the job I was doing. Grocery clerk, cotton picker, garbage truck. I got a picture of that one, posing against the truck with three of my buddies. Mailed her the picture. I kept that up for about four years—till I finally settled on butchering. Then I sent her pictures of me standing by the meatblock till I was sure she got the point—then I quit writing. Never wrote again. That's the story, boy. Why ain't you laughing? It's pretty funny, isn't it?

[Published by Dramatists Play Service]

'ROUND MIDNIGHT
by Laura Harrington

On this night Leo and Sal are seeing each other for the first time in five years. Leo and Sal were lovers in the past, but they are pretending that they are strangers meeting for the first time. In this monologue, Leo tells Sal the story of their love affair as though it had happened to someone else.

LEO: I had this girl once . . .

She had this angel face, but you'd strip her down and there she'd be with this angel face and black panties.

I used to want to rip her skin—and protect her—hold her so tender. She'd feel so small in my hands, like her chest would break right open from her heart pounding so hard.

Hot summer nights I'd watch her sleep.

I'd get out of bed and sit in a chair so I could see her better.

Her skin glowed. Real soft, a sheen.

And she smelled so sweet.

(*Beat.*)

She made me feel like she would give me anything she had.

She gave with both hands. Flat out. Anything I wanted.

Nothing scared her . . .

I felt like a starving man.

My eyes ached, my belly ached with wanting her.

And the more she gave to me . . .

I wanted her skin.

I wanted to be closer than skin.

If I could just rip her open wide enough, enter her deep enough.

Fill her, just fill her . . .

Anything so I could hold her.

Anything so I could make her mine.

[Available at New Dramatists]

OPENING DAY
by Willy Holtzman

Zeke (Daddy) Zweiker owns a hog farm in southeastern Missouri. Several years before the action of the play, he sold off a piece of his land to the federal government, which used it as a site for a missile silo.

Daddy is a composite of two separate encounters. One, with a man who was dying of brain cancer and who had decided that he could forestall death by staying awake. The other, with a farmer who wanted to leave his land to his family but was ashamed that the land contained a Minuteman missile site. The character, Daddy, is a man who has accepted death, but cannot accept the horribly wrong legacy he will leave.

DADDY: When they first dug at the site, dug down, deep down, they found bones. First cow bones, then man bones, then injun bones . . . dinosaur bones! Can you hear 'em? Chickachickachickachicka. Hear 'em rattlin'. A graveyard—that's all the world is, a graveyard. So that there missile silo's right where it oughta be. It's in the design of things. "Silo?" Hell. A funnel. A goddamn funnel to eternity. Try and plug up the funnel with a atom. A little bitty old atom, with all that power and harm. A whole thing, you see. A whole thing that don't come apart except with fury. Like a heart. A human heart. Yep, the site's where it oughta be—on a pile of bones. The world's a bone in the ear of the Almighty . . . or a flea.

Back, way back. Back. The injuns would take a white man in a raid. Take him as their own. And summon his injun ways. The injun's in all of us, hidden in a small corner of the soul, full of magic and wonder and instinct and nature. Naturally we hate injuns 'cause we fear the hidden part of us . . . the art of us. Anyways, the injuns would hold onto that white man till the white went out of him and the savage come in, the way a hog grows tusky when you turn him loose in the wild. That white man would become an injun, and live an injun, and die an injun, though being an injun he wouldn't so much draw the line between life and death. But every so often, injuns'd turn a white man loose. He'd come back to the white men, but he could never come back to white man ways. 'Cause he'd seen the injun in him, and he knew we all bend to the same seasons and tides and the bones under our feet. He knew we were just another animal on God's green earth and not God himself. No more than a stone is God, and maybe less. And the white man can kill an injun, kill every last injun. But he can't kill the injun in him, 'less he kills himself. And so there are missiles.

Death took me nigh three weeks ago. Took me while I slept. And for some reason, death turned me loose again. Like the injun turned the white man loose. To know death is in all of us, and you can't escape it. It's part of us to the bone, the bone in the ear of God. And it is not terrible—one at a time. All at once? It's . . . unthinkable. Now, I got to think on it. Undo what I done. Plug up the silo. Hold back eternity. Can't sleep till I done it. You go to sleep, my friend. I don't dare, just yet. Dream for two.

[Available at New Dramatists]

A SINGULAR KINDA GUY
by David Ives

A young guy is out on a Saturday night in his best shoes, talking to a girl he's met in a bar. She's nice, he likes her. But he's got this sort of a confession, see. There's something she ought to know about him. And he's never told this to anybody. You see, on the inside, deep on the inside, he isn't really a guy at all. He's an Olivetti electric self-correcting typewriter. And he can't even type!

MITCH: I know what you're thinking. You're looking at me and you're saying to yourself: average guy. Normal human being. Nothing out of the ordinary. Well, that's what I thought too for lots of years, and boy, was I wrong.

Now I look back, I think I always really knew the truth about myself, underneath. It's like, sometimes I'd look in the mirror in the morning and I'd get this weird feeling like what I was looking at was not what I really was looking at? Or else I'd be standing in a crowd of people at a party, and suddenly I'd get this idea like I was standing in a huge empty space and there wasn't anybody around me for miles. Episodes of "vastation," if you know that beautiful word. And then one day I had a . . . I don't know what you'd call it. A mystical experience?

I was walking down Lex over in the thirties when I go by this office supply shop. Just a crummy little place. But I turn and I look and I see . . . an Olivetti model 250 portable electric typewriter. Are you familiar with that particular model? Have you ever seen the old Olivetti 250? Well let me tell you—it's sublime. The lines. The shape. The slant of the keyboard. It's all there! It's a thing of beauty!

Anyway, I'm standing there looking at this thing, and it's like I recognize it from someplace. It's like I'm looking at family somehow, like I'm seeing some long-lost older brother for the first time, and suddenly I realize: That's me, right there. That thing in the window is exactly what I feel like, on the inside. Same lines, same shape, same aesthetic. And what I realized was: I . . . am a typewriter. No, really! A typewriter! All those years I thought I was a human being, on the inside I was really a portable Olivetti 250 with automatic correctibility. And you know what? I can't even type.

Well, needless to say, this revelation came as a shock. But all of a sudden it's clear to me how come I always got off on big words—like "vastation." Or phenomenological. Or subcutaneous. Words are what a typewriter's all about, right?

Problem is, it can be a lonely thing, being a typewriter in a world of human beings. And now here I am being replaced every day by word processors. You know, last week on the news I heard some guy say that in ten years typewriters will be totally obsolete?

Here I finally figure out what I really am, and suddenly I'm half an antique already.

Plus, there's my love life, which is problematical to say the least. The difficulties involved in a typewriter finding a suitable partner in this town can be pretty prodigious, as you can imagine. At least now I know how come I always loved—not just sex, sex is anywhere —but . . . touch. Being touched, and touching. Being touched is part of the nature and purpose of typewriters, that's how we express ourselves and the human person along with us. Hands on the keyboard and the right touch—fire away.

Women's hands. They're practically the first thing I notice. Nice set of shapely fingers. Good manicure. No hangnails. Soft skin. I'm not a finger fetishist or anything, you understand, it's just . . .

You've got a pretty nice pair of hands yourself, there. That's what I noticed, that's how come I stepped over here to talk to you. I know that sounds pretty loony, but you know I never told anybody this before? Somehow I just felt like I could trust you, and . . .

What, I beg your pardon?

I don't understand.

You're not really a girl? Sure, you're a girl, you're a beautiful girl, so . . .

You're what? You're actually a sheet of paper? Ten-pound bond? Ivory tinted? Pure cotton fiber?

(MITCH *holds out his hand.*)

Glad to meet you.

[Available at New Dramatists]

NIGHTCOIL
by Jeffrey M. Jones

It is forbidden to sing, and Old Man Moses, a compulsive singer, has been chased and caught by four men for this crime. They order him to talk, and in an attempt to ingratiate himself with them and forestall his inevitable punishment, he delivers the following speech. Unfortunately, it becomes apparent that his memory isn't all that it should be.

OLD MAN MOSES (*Discovered on stage with his pants off.*): Ah yes (ahem . . .)

Hello! . . .

Well, well, you seem to have caught me with my (what an embarrassment . . .)

I . . . (uh) . . . Oh, dear . . . I . . . well . . . I . . .

All right, all right, all right,

I'll talk, I'll talk, don't hurt me please, I'll talk, I will, I really will . . .

I really will . . .

I'll talk . . .

Okay?

Huh?

Look, gimme a minute, will you?

I mean, these things don't im*med*iately come to mind, you know.

(You know? . . .)

(You don't know . . . oh, well . . .)

Now, let me see—how does it go?

No, that's not it: The umpy-pumpy-piddly-pum . . .

Hmmmmm . . .

So where was I?

Ah, yes!

Ahem!

To be, or something-or-other—

That is the . . . something-or-other . . .

Now I know that's not quite right, not quite right yet . . .

Hmmmmmmmmm . . .

To be or not to be . . .

To be or not to be . . .

To be or not to be or not to be

Or not to shuffle—

Aye, there's the rub!

That is . . . the rub! (no)

That is . . . the consummation (no)

("the mortal coil"—that's in there somewhere . . .)

That is . . . the question! Aye!

The question!

Whether 'tis nobler in the mortal coil—no, no—the mind,

Nobler in the mind . . .

(Now let me see . . .)

Whether 'tis nobler in the mind . . .

To grunt and sweat under a weary load (that can't be right)

Whether 'tis nobler in the mind

To take up arms against outrageous fortune or . . . .

Seeking his quietus or . . . to seek . . .

Or his quietus make with a bare bodkin and by opposing end the . . .

That is the contumely that makes consolation of so long life or something like that.

For *who* (thou Philistine!) would fardels bear—aye, there's the rub,

Who would grunt and sweat under a heavy load but that the thought of something after death, that undiscovered bourne—

No wait, go back!

To die! To sleep! No more!

(I've got it!)

'Tis a consummation devoutly to be wished: to die—perchance to sleep—perchance to sleep—perchance to dream—perchance to dream—perchance to be—perchance to shuffle—

Aye, there's the rub!

There's the something-or-other (I forgot) must give us pause . . .

For, in that sleep of death what dreams may come when we have shuffled off this mortal coil (that's where it goes)

The perturbation and the thousand natural shocks
the flesh is heir to—
   The whips and scorns!
   The slings and arrows!
   The something-or-other's something-or-other and the
proud man's contumely
   Must give us pause!

   What's he to Hecuba?
   Aye, there's the rub!
   (*Sings.*) "Way down upon the Swaneeeeeeee Rivahh-
hhhhh . . ."
   (OLD MAN MOSES *runs off the stage.*)

[Published by P.A.J. Publications in *Wordplays IV*]

AN AUDIBLE SIGH
by Lee Kalcheim

Gale McGee is an outrageous writer, newly married and living for the summer with his wife's family. He finds himself being criticised for not acting like a responsible husband, particularly when his wife brings up the idea of having a baby.

GALE: Responsible??? What are you talking responsible? It's easy to be responsible. I've written half a dozen novels. With no help. And after the first successful one . . . every one was harder. It's a big responsibility living up to yourself . . . But I managed to do it. And when I couldn't do it as well . . . I turned out twenty pages of drek a day in Hollywood . . . Drunk, sober, gassed, I turned them in . . . Big, responsible me. I'm responsible for getting this newspaper out. It's all mine. No one to help. Am I afraid? No. Do I shudder? No . . . Do I shirk my responsibility? No. I love it. I'm dying to get this paper out. I'll do anything. I'll take all the credit, all the blame . . . bear all the troubles. This is my baby. I'm responsible. And you use that stupid argument that I've heard a thousand times . . . to try to get me to do something I don't want to do! It's as if someone were to walk in that door and say, Mr. McGee, I want you to be in charge of the local Girl Scout troop. And I'd say, no, I don't want to. And he'd say, ah ha, you don't want responsibility. And I'd say, No . . . I just hate Girl Scouts. And even if I loved Girl Scouts, I just don't have the time.

Christ, what kind of a world would this be without the irresponsible? Where would we be without the followers? We'd have millions of leaders . . . with no one to take care of! They—they told Gaugin he was irresponsible when he went to Tahiti . . . and what did "they" ever do for the world?

Honey, I'm forty now. By all rights it's the perfect time for me to have children. I, in fact, should have had them years ago. But "should" is one word I detest. Because "should" is a standard setup by other people. You should get married, you should have children, you should . . .

I think, I think . . . that's what I admired so much about "Bulldog." He knew exactly what was good for him. He needed no one, and he was really able to be alone. You see . . . he'd go to class and he'd give this lecture . . . put everything into it . . . He was really getting juiced on his students . . . and then . . . he'd drive out of New Haven, in this beat-up car . . . and he'd drive out to the sticks of Connecticut. And he'd go up to his little house and just hole up again. Otherwise, he never saw anyone. Or spoke to anyone. He just . . . saved it all . . . for the kids. I couldn't swallow it all. This man was ecstatic . . . Not happy. Ecstatic! Then off to the sticks. Poof. To no one.

(GALE *sings.*)

"Bulldog . . . Bulldog . . . Bow wow wow . . . Eli Yale." The guys used to sing when he drove by. "Bulldog, Bulldog . . . Bow wow wow . . . Eeeeee Liiiii Yale!"

[Available at New Dramatists]

BREAKFAST WITH LES AND BESS
by Lee Kalcheim

Les is a sportswriter who hasn't been writing for several years. He and his wife are a successful radio couple. When he gets a job offer to broadcast ball games for the new Houston baseball team (it's 1962), he's excited. He wants to get back to work again and give up the ridiculous show. Bess, his wife, resists. Home, drunk after a party, he confronts her.

LES: Bess! My beeaautiful Bess. My lovely Bess. I'm asking you to start over with me. Remember how much fun it was when I was a hardworking sports columnist and you were a gung-ho political reporter? If that damn gossip columnist on the *News* hadn't gotten sick, you'd probably have six Pulitzer prizes by now. Whatever you do, you do well. You got a job to write schlock and you wrote schlock so well . . . you're still writing it. And we've been broadcasting it for ten years! But, Bess . . . this is our opportunity. We can go back. We can—we can . . . erase all the success that has made us so miserable and go back and be excited about our work again. Remember how excited we were? Remember the breakfast we had with Mayor LaGuardia when he thanked you for dogging him about the Harlem housing projects. That was exciting. Remember when we flew to Chicago in '48 to watch the Eagles–Cardinals football final in the blinding snowstorm? With one-eyed Tommy Thompson . . . the Eagles quarterback . . . trying to find his receivers . . . and we're sitting there in the stands with our hands in hot chocolate! We were excited about everything. And each other. Look at us now. You are the world's busiest woman. I am the world's most unmotivated man. Look . . . I've got a proposal. I'll . . . go to Texas . . . I'll take this job. You come down . . . for a while. Take a leave of absence. You could do that. Just look the place over. You'll probably love it. I mean . . . we could get some . . . adobe house out in the desert. You'd have a place out in the sun to sit and work on that book you always wanted to write . . . about America's crazy love affair with celebrities—what was that . . . "American Royalty." You used to talk about that book all the time . . . that was a great idea . . . so . . . you could sit out there at a nice . . . big picnic table . . . and I'd come home from the ball games . . . and cook up a barbeque dinner . . . and we'd have friends over . . . two or three friends, like normal people . . . and we'd sit out late . . . and look up at the sky . . . and talk . . . and . . . do all the dumb things ordinary people do. We've tried everything else. Let's try this! I loved you once . . . and you were nuts about me . . . We wanted to be important writers. And we loved that dream. You know what we are now? Famous. We're famous. That's all. We're lousy parents. Lousy, lousy lovers, but famous . . .

[Published by Samuel French]

FRIENDS
by Lee Kalcheim

Mel is living alone in a cabin in Vermont, trying to get his life together. His best friend, Okie, a successful assistant ambassador at the U.N., has come to visit. Mel (a gourmet cook) dives into making dinner for his friend, and pours out the seriocomic history that has led him to this place.

MEL: I keep hoping. The next thing I do will click. That's why I got the cabin. I took it last summer. And I started drawing again. And I was really kind of high. So I quit the teaching job. And the *Voice* picked up the cartoon. And I said, I'm on my way! And then . . . I'm up here. Alone. Turning out one strip a week. And it starts getting to me. And I'm not high anymore. One strip a week and I can't come up with anything. And . . . my social life is for shit. I've gone through the local single schoolteachers. And the divorced housewives. I'm starting on the married ones now. I swear to God . . . some redneck Downeast husband is gonna catch me and blow a hole in my head. (*Headlines*) "New York Gourmet Cartoonist Murdered in Vermont Cabin!"

I've got a two-year lease here. I'm going to see it through. I gotta give this a chance. Part of succeeding is perseverence.

Y'see, *my* father never pushed me about my life. He was afraid to ask . . . one of those complicated, screwed-up successful Jews. By the time I started working, he'd been made a judge. He was so goddamn *fair*.

He was sooo damn patient. "The Judge." He never said straight out, "What the hell are you doing with your life? Stop screwing around and do something." That would have been a relief. I saw it in his eyes every time, but he never said it. Instead he'd say, "What are you up to?" I'd say, "I'm a pastry chef in a restaurant." He'd say, "Oh, that's interesting." But his eyes would say, "What the hell are you doing?" My brother's the big success. Plastic surgeon in L.A. My brother's done nose jobs for a lot of those starlets. Every so often he'll call me up and tell me I have to watch something on television. "One of my noses is on a movie at nine o'clock!"

He's got a Bel Air home with a pool and a sauna and a pretty bitchy wife. Plays tennis everyday. Drives one of his three Mercedes. Shit, he couldn't please my father either. My father wanted him to cure cancer. Never said it to him. But I knew.

My brother didn't know. He's happy. He's too dumb not to be happy.

It's the smarties like us that get in trouble. We think too much. That's why I got this cabin. I figured I'd get away from everything that's been a destructive influence in my life. Intelligent people. Racy surroundings.

Good-looking women. So here I am in the mountains. It's quiet. The people are simple. The women are ugly. And I'm fuckin' miserable.

[Available at New Dramatists]

IS THERE LIFE AFTER HIGH SCHOOL
Book by Jeff Kindley

The setting is a high school gymnasium and the plot revolves around the lives of people who are ten years older than they were in high school, but not so very much older at all in terms of their emotional lives.

JIM WANAMAKER: I had a dream last night where someone found out I never took these courses that were necessary for graduation, and I had to go back to school to make up the work. I sat down at a desk which was way too small for me, but nobody else in the classroom seemed to notice that I was any different from them. Then Mrs. Delaney—my American Problems teacher—hands out these test booklets, and I look at the cover and someone has drawn obscene pictures all over it. I don't know what to do. Should I tell Mrs. Delaney, and call attention to myself, or should I just ignore the pictures?—in which case she'll probably think I drew them. The pictures are in pencil, see, so I start to erase them. All of these little breasts and penises and stick people doing horrible things to each other. But as soon as I get one part erased, I notice another one—and another. Finally the bell rings and Mrs. Delaney starts collecting the booklets, and I realize I never even opened mine. I don't even know what the test was about. And what's worse, all the pictures are still there. I start tearing up the booklet like crazy and sticking pieces of it in my mouth, trying to chew it all up and swallow it before she gets to me. Then she's standing over me and she says, "Where's your booklet, James? What have you done with it?" That's as far as it went. I woke up in a cold sweat. I'd wanted to say, "I ate it, you bitch! I ate it!"—but I never talked back to Mrs. Delaney in my life.

[Published by Samuel French]

THE 72-OUNCE STEAK
by Sherry Kramer

Brent is a truck driver. He is uneducated but not unintelligent. He picks up hitchhikers along the road, and finds that if he listens to their stories carefully, he always learns something interesting. At present, he is accompanied by a particularly interesting rider, a banker who is hitching his way to get hitched, as his last macho fling before getting married.

Brent has just thrown up after eating the 72-ounce steak and all the trimmings prior to telling his story. He is in the living room of a woman who lives next to the steak house, a woman who he slept with once, a year before, and who he knows, from stories on the road, is desperately in love with him. He is very proud of his triumph over the steak. It will be a cruel moment when he realizes that the woman he is telling it to has heard the exact same story dozens of times.

BRENT: You let them know, right when you walk in under the big cow, through the swinging doors, so they give you the special table. It's the best table in the house. You get your own waiter too.

As soon as you sit down you have to sign this

release. I guess they've had guys croak on them, choking on a piece of meat. They've got this real sharp knife hanging on the wall behind the table, and the maitre d' knows how to use it in an emergency, so you have to sign this release saying if he botches it, if he tries to save you and he botches it, you agree not to sue.

I guess their normal restaurant insurance covers them if you strangle eating a normal dinner, on your own.

You got to eat the 72-ounce steak, the tossed salad, the shrimp cocktail, the vegetable medley, the twice-baked potato, and the pie à la mode, all in an hour.

You eat it all in an hour, you don't have to pay.

You get it down, they carve your name with a branding iron on a big wooden plaque.

They show you the rules: No talking to customers at other tables. No eating on the floor. No throwing up. Your waiter accompanies you to the john and I mean accompanies. They got a large stall built special. He watches you like a hawk. Checks the toilet paper when you blow your nose. You throw up even a little bit, you got to pay.

You also got to pay you want anything other than coffee or tea, like a Coke or something.

They let you order it any way you want. They ask you, do you want it rare. Medium rare. Raw. Well. I ordered it extra well. I mean you go to McDonalds, you get a quarter pounder, that's a quarter pounder before cooking, right, and what do you get, you get nothing, right? So I figured, seventy-two times ounces, that's four and a half pounds, that's eighteen times nothing.

The waiter made this funny face when he took my order.

I got comfortable at the table. I made sure everything was as it should be. I tested the steak knife hanging on the wall behind me. It was sharp, all right. It was something like a surgeon would use. It was much sharper than the knife next to my plate.

The platter hit the table. In that instant I developed my strategy. I would cut the steak into fourths, and eat one fourth at the top of every quarter. I would finish out the rest of the time in the side dishes. The waiter, who was clocking me with a large stopwatch— and a true professional, I might add—graciously agreed to sound a small bell at appropriate intervals.

I picked up my fork and my knife.

You talk about your fatal errors. You talk about your fatal flaws. Everybody has them.

Seventy-two ounces of shoe leather. Seventy-two ounces of gristle and fat and flesh, charred beyond recognition. Seventy-two ounces of open-hearthed, pet-rified prime. I tossed my knife and fork over my shoulder. They were as good as useless to me now.

I was able to rip the thing in half. I had to stand up to do it—they let you stand up. I was reminded, and inspired, by a painting I once saw of Jacob wrestling with the angel. It was a lot like that.

That funny look was pity.

I started chewing on the larger half. I wanted to give myself an edge. My waiter sounded the first quarter. I'd barely made it past the outer crust on the pointed end. I started to panic. The waiter reached across and wiped my forehead with the napkin he had draped over his arm. I'd never actually seen a waiter use the napkin they've always got draped over their arms, so I was doubly grateful.

I realized I needed a psychological boost here, something to keep me going, give me hope. The shrimp cocktail caught my eye. It was only four jumbo gulf shrimp, drenched in a plentiful helping of sauce. I reached for my fork—it's hard to break the habits of a lifetime—then picked up the dish and tossed it back. I could feel the shrimp gliding, coasting down my throat. Once again I nodded at my waiter. I felt sure the extra sauce had been his doing.

I took up the chunk of meat in my hands. I dove into it, buried my face in it, determined to eat my way through to the light.

The bell rang. It had a far-off sound, as if it were coming from another world. I stayed where I was, chewing, ripping, swallowing, submerged. Again the bell. Fifteen minutes left. I stuffed the rest of the flesh down my throat. I gagged, kept on swallowing, come on, come on, you can do it. My fists struck the table. *One. Two.* I was in trouble. I saw my waiter glancing nervously in the direction of the razor-sharp steak knife. *Three*!!! I got it down. I took a deep, beautiful breath.

"Close call," my waiter said. We both looked at the knife hanging on the wall behind me.

I jumped up. My hand snaked out, reaching the knife an instant before his did. I tore if off the wall. Our eyes met.

"My decision," I said.

I was able to slash the remaining half of the steak into eight slices before the knife gave out. I ate one of them. Then two. Then three. The tossed salad. That looks easy. Sure, that will go down, all that dressing.

Two handfuls, in, swallow, can't feel it going down, that feels good. Two pieces of meat, don't chew, no time to chew, just swallow, swallow. *Damn you, swallow*. Another. Swallow. Another.

(BRENT *panting, looks around, disoriented*.)

The baked potato. Yes. Won't fit. *Won't fit*. Tear it in half.

Vegetables. Don't forget your vegetables.

Okay. Okay. What? What?

(*Despair*.)

One minute? One?

(*Hysterical*.)

One minute! Apple pie—where's that bitch—that apple pie—Jesus Christ—*Thirty seconds?* Two slices left—swallow, swallow—fifteen seconds—one piece left, one—(BRENT *choking, gagging*.)—get it in—*get it in! swallow!!!* Five seconds—five—four—three—two—one —*swallow!!!*

The bell!!! The bell!!!

The waiter slammed me up against the wall and pinned me while the maitre d' pried my mouth open and looked inside with a flashlight. But I was clean. It was every bit of it gone.

They frisked me quickly, quietly, efficiently. They knew their business. Mac McClellan himself came over to congratulate me. My waiter hugged me, and went off to heat up the branding iron.

They blew the whistle, so everybody stopped eating during the engraving ceremony, and when it was over, everybody cheered.

Now I ask you. Have you ever heard a story like that before?

[Available at New Dramatists]

THE WALL OF WATER
by *Sherry Kramer*

It's John's first day on the job as a psychotherapeutic nurse. He graduated just this morning from his training program, and is the worst in his class. He is only dimly aware of this. He has been sent out to take care of a patient having a complete psychic breakdown. By mistake, he has been given directions to the wrong room, and has sedated and restrained the wrong woman. He is the perfect example of "A little knowledge is a dangerous thing." He is in the bathroom, speaking directly to the audience over his shoulder during this monologue. He is masked from the waist down by a tile partition, urinating.

JOHN: I know about muscles. I've been taught. And the first thing they teach people about muscles is about the one muscle in the body that can't be taught. It can be trained, a bit. But it can't be improved. You can't make it grow, and isn't that what muscle work is all about? Growth? Expansion? Lifting one hundred fifty pounds today. One hundred fifty-one pounds tomorrow. That's the thing about muscles. They benefit from exercise. All except one.

There is one lone muscle that becomes, with exercise, with practice, not stronger, but weaker. It is the muscle that is trickling your life away. Ohhh, not the heart, you're thinking it's the heart but it's not. The heart can learn things. The heart can grow. The heart can be brought back from a month in the country healthier, robust, strong.

The bladder, however, is brought back from a month in the country just another month older. Another month closer to the inevitable irreparable disrepair.

The bladder grows, all right, from practice. It grows weaker. It does not benefit from the one exercise it receives—holding it in—but perversely becomes less able to hold it in the more prolonged and frequently holding it in occurs.

I can't tell you what a comfort this piece of information has been to me.

You know what it's like. You're walking down the street, you think you're looking pretty sharp. Maybe the checkout clerk at the Seven–Eleven was nice to you, and your mood just swings up, and your whole day is set. Maybe, if the checkout clerk was nice enough, or pretty enough, you even kinda believe in God. In a way. So anyway, you're feeling good, you're looking good, and then some guy walks past that has muscles that make you look like a worm and you get that ache in your stomach and that ache starts eating you up and it doesn't stop with you it starts eating up your whole entire day and the existence of God, maybe, too.

That's when I remember about that little muscle. Because when that guy walks past me, and that ache begins its business, and I start to turn into a worm, I just say—under my breath, of course—"Hey, buddy. Your arms may be the size of my thighs. Your thighs may be the size of my waist. But you can pump iron till the cows come home—that little muscle that controls your bladder is still the same size as mine. When you gotta go, buddy, you gotta go, and when you step up to the stall, buddy, we are equal."

And I walk by with my head held up a little higher. And that ache in my stomach just dies away. I walk past that muscle-bound, Nautilus-loving towelbrain with my humanity, and even occasionally, my belief in God, intact.

[Available at New Dramatists]

LOOK AT ANY MAN
by Harding Lemay

Earl, a former child movie star, is now a handsome
thirty-five-year-old man. He is destitute, black, and
married to a woman named Luella. Marian, a popular
author of biographies, invites Earl and his wife to
come to New York City so he can tell her his story for
a new book. Earl recounts the miserable life he led as
a young teenager traveling across the country.

EARL: I was a nice little chocolate dumpling ...
(*Laughs nervously.*). There were guys who liked little
boys, especially little black boys like me . . . Later on,
I found out about girls but first . . . Well, you was
asking about when I was riding the rails . . .
   Coasting along in boxcars every night, broke and
hungry and cold. And in the dark, when the doors slid
open, guys got in, one, two, maybe more, and the
doors closed up again, and the train took off across
the country. And they found me, sleeping in the corner, or just staring at them. The night got cold, and I
was hungry. Christ, the things you do because you're
cold . . . and hungry! The things people ask you to do!
The things people do to you! And the same old smells

came back, the smell of piss, and vomit flooding up against my teeth, until I sneaked away to my corner, my legs all wet, and sticky, and their faces staring at me in the dark—white faces—staring at me but not seeing me, and whispering to themselves. Then the train stops and the doors open again. Some get off and some get on. Then, all over again, for pennies, and quarters, nickels, and dimes . . . and wine, and liquor, and something to eat. And in the dark, hands all over my freezing bones, smelly, smothering breaths on my face.

[Available at New Dramatists]

SAVONAROLA
by Romulus Linney

No one frightened his listeners as did this fifteenth-century Italian monk, until he fell victim to the passions he had aroused, and was buried alive by them.

(SAVONAROLA appears in his black-hooded friar's robe, standing in a Florentine pulpit of carved wood, thrust forward.)

SAVONAROLA: *What were you then, when I came to you?*

(*Pause.*)

Sin you had forgotten. That word meant nothing to you. It was replaced, in a golden age, by fulfillment. That was your word then. The City lived for that.

(SAVONAROLA *smiles, nods.*)

Well, why not? The City was rich. Its bankers the saviors of the world.

(*Pause.*)

The City was strong. Its armies possessors of great weapons, invented by the brilliant men whose minds all that money had set free.

(*Pause.*)

The City was wise. It was ruled by a prince not even Plato, whom everyone went about reading, would fault. He was a wonder. Judge, soldier, farmer, banker, poet, architect, splendid, healthy, brilliant animal man, glorious in both the spirit and the flesh. He was called "Magnificence."

(*Pause.*)

The City was pious. In gigantic buildings the God of its Fathers was worshipped. With mighty hymns rising to heaven.

(*Pause.*)

And the City was beautiful. Its people stood enraptured, gazing at themselves embodied in paintings skillful beyond all description in giving back to mankind the ancient beauty of his flesh. And the women, no longer buried in shrouds, rose from the sea in those paintings, slept on clouds, and danced in flowing robes to winds of spring.

(*Pause.*)

And then I came to you. Harsh, ugly friar, with his homely face and hoarse voice, his hairshirt and black robe, and what did I tell you?

(*Pause.* SAVONAROLA *gathers himself.*)

I told you you were not rich, you were poor. I told you you were not strong, you were weak. Not wise but stupid, not pious but pagan and not beautiful at all. You were not a City. You were a cesspool, and your brilliant colors to me were shit.

Is a woman beautiful, her breast naked, pawed by a child and called Mary? You paint the Mother of God in a whore's body with a whore's tits and you paint Jesus Christ playing with them! Look what you are doing! That is not the body of a man painted for the glory of

God! That is the body of a fool, painted for the plea-
sure of a Sodomite! Look, I told you! Look at your-
selves! A sword hangs over you, descending upon you!
You will be destroyed!

(Pause.)

And what happened? Your prince, your Magnificence? Aged forty-three, his brain burned with fever,
and he died in agony. From the north, invaders came,
and your soldiers threw down their arms, cowards
every man. The bankers gave away the City's money
to save their skins, the citizens' congress dissolved
itself and ran away, even the Holy Church turned
from you, into its own corruption, *and I said it would*
all happen! It did, and your great city under the hand
of a righteous wrathful God became Sodom, became
Gomorrah, became at last, itself!

(Pause.)

And then you called for me. Together we ruled, in
modesty and simplicity. Fulfillment was obedience to
the will of God.

(Pause. Upon him and around him we see the reflec-
tions of fire. SAVONAROLA *smiles.)*

In those days, you did well. But you tired, as humans do, of your virtue. I am not sure exactly when. I
think it was that day together, we burned in a great
pire at the center of the City, the vanities of life:
the mirrors, the rouge, the wigs, the gowns and furs, the
cards, the indecent paintings, the heathen books. The
sight of that fire you could not bear, and you turned
toward me.

(Pause. SAVONAROLA *speaks softly and gently.)*

And now, at the center of you, in your square of
carnivals and worship, you will burn me, O my City.

My flesh will hang melting in red-hot manacles. Children will throw rocks to bring down my bones. You could not, at this stage of your climb to God, tolerate the truth about yourselves very long. But I will always love you, and I will always be ready to come to you and speak the truth to you. I know that on a day not far distant from this, the one when you burn me, you will need me again. You will call for me, and I will be ready to come to you once more.

(SAVONAROLA *leaves the pulpit.*)

[Available at New Dramatists]

CHINA WARS
by Robert Lord

Hal, a man in his mid-thirties, has recently married for the third time. With his wife, Ianthe, he has left the sophisticated fast-paced city where he used to live and thrive, to begin a new life in a small village in a remote corner of New England.

In the monologue, Hal is talking to Ken, his next-door neighbor. It is their first meeting. Hal is full of enthusiasm for his new beginning.

HAL: This is all so exciting it's hard for me to put it into words. Last night was our first night in our new house. It was one of the first nights of our marriage. It was a night of new beginnings. Of fresh starts. Ianthe (my dear, sweet, angelic, third and last wife) Ianthe and I wandered around our barely furnished house and discussed and planned—the gymnasium, the Jacuzzi, the sauna, the swimming pool, the extra garage, and the new wing. The new wing will be flawless. A large, wood-paneled billiard room for me and a gallery with Ionian columns and marble floors where we can display Ianthe's paintings. She's a wonderful artist. She has painted me on numerous occasions. Often nude with my muscles oiled. She finds my body has appealing symmetry.

Last night we stayed up late drinking Remy Martin by candlelight. Finally, at about two or three in the morning, I turned to Ianthe, I grabbed her delicate, fragile body in these strong, masculine hands. I picked her up and carried her to our bedroom. I laid her gently on the bed and then covered her entire body with hot, passionate kisses. It wasn't long before my flawless technique brought her to a fever pitch of erotic desire. I plunged deep inside her. We rocked back and forth for hours. When she climaxed for the eighteenth or nineteenth time (I lost count) I shuddered and shot my wad. We collapsed sweaty and exhausted on the pink satin sheets. It was but a moment or two before Ianthe fell into a deep, deep sleep. I heard her breathing change and that gentle, soft whistling sound she makes. Does your wife whistle?

(HAL *makes a breathy, whistling sound.*)

It was so perfect I couldn't still my heart. My physical body was spent, but I was still alive and passionate. And I thought to myself: "Hal, this is your fresh start!" What a feeling. All the leaves turned over. All the possibility. All the chances. I was in a world where anything was possible. Where bad didn't exist. Where hope was real and palpable. Hope was surrounding me. Caressing me. Holding me. My body was electric with . . . with . . . with . . . And then I too fell asleep. And my dream. My sweet, sweet dream, of mown lawns, herbaceous borders, of rocking chairs on summer porches. Of mailmen and barbershops, town meetings and patriotic parades. I haven't dreamt like that . . . Not for . . . not since . . . maybe never.

[Available at New Dramatists]

UNTITLED (THE DARK AGES FLAT OUT)
by Matthew Maguire

This play is about a man writing a play, about a man going blind who sees with his mind a play about the fear of blindness and the paradox of clarity. This monologue, "I panic and go catatonic" is a description of one aspect of the creative act. It is a story of how anyone who attempts to create (writer, composer, painter, actor), must wrestle with an infinite number of conflicting voices. It is comic but not without its frightening aspect. [Track 1 can be performed alone. If the actor wanted to also include Track 1A and 1B then he/she could record them on cassette tape and cue them at the right moments.]

Track 1
I Panic and go Catatonic

I clutch. I get the shakes. I clench my jaw like a steel trap. I panic that all the voices in my head will speak to me at once, and I'll stop moving and speaking because I get sucked right into their world. I get the willies. The screamin' bejesies. These voices start going, one at a time they mount up, immense, blinding harangues. I'm shittin' stagefright. My eyes are popping right out of my head and my hair is dropping out in clumps to the floor and my voices are silencing me. My gears disengage and the mind released from the tongue spins faster and faster. Tongue no longer fast enough to keep up I turn to the pressing dialogues, trialogues mounting up inside. Telepathic now. I speak to everyone around me torrents of words you see no motion lips do not twitch. It is not nothing. It is everything. Catatonia uncontained. Mind has track bleed all tracks talking at *once*. Mind cooling rapidly from acceleration without friction from cranial *prison*. Mind spinning acrobatically. Everything at once. Mind drops to sinkhole trace collecting every thought that doesn't belong anyplace else. I go ambient. A fine line at which the play stops focusing the gaze and concentrates on filling the room. Can many diffused focal points create an ambient atmosphere? Is it possible not to have a focus? Is this a lie. It's not right, is it, that the mouth cannot speak as fast as the mind thinks? I go serial. Short installments at regular intervals arranged in successive parts. I seriate. Diptychs, triptychs, octotychs, nonotychs, never one thing, always many things. I syncopate and am constantly accelerating, constantly accelerating, constantly accelerating, constantly accelerating!

Track 1A

I panic because nothing will come out if it has to come out one at a time. What if you have to understand it one at a time? What if it's in the wrong sequence? What if it's never understood? What if I have aphasia? What if I'm invisible? What if panic is the only creative state? I panic that my mind will flop around like a fish on a hot dock. Like a fish on a hot dock.

Track 1B

I define play. Play as collage. Play as a way of spending time. Play as altered state. Play as environment. Play as story. Play as mixed-media assemblage. Play as entertainment. Play as charting thought. Play as sharing information. Play as a reassurance of the present. Play as the Dreamtime. Play as landscape. Play as structured time. Play as meditation. Play as the panic state. Play as testimony. Play as memory. Play as tantrum. Play as moving text. Play as the loss of control. Play as dialectic. Play as the movement of light. Play as portrait. Play as vision. Play as confession. Play as hallucination. Play as defecation. Play as mask. Play as the room. Play as political outcry. Play as the live communication of an idea.

[Available at New Dramatists]

SPLIT SECOND
by Dennis McIntyre

The story is a simple one. A policeman named Val shoots a suspect in a burglary. The policeman is black, the victim, white. Against the advice of his retired policeman father, his best friend on the force, his wife, Alea, and everyone else he confronts, the black policeman cannot come to grips with simply lying and letting the matter rest.

VAL: What else was there? I grew up with cops. The only people who ever came over to our house were cops. Cops and cops' wives. Cops and cops' kids. And once in a while, a real distinction—some goddamned prosecutor who should have been a cop! Lloyd, Frank, Daryll, every partner you ever had!

And you loved it! Being a cop, that was special. The world couldn't get along without cops. In fact, cops ruled the world. That's how society functioned. I remember, Mom and me, we must have spent two thousand hours waiting for you to change your goddamn uniform. And where in the hell were you? Drinking your Rolling Rock with the boys, that's where you were. Cleaning your gun, loading it, unloading it—

But where were we, Mom and me? Out front, waiting, watching the hookers get booked. Or the guy who'd just carved up his wife with a screwdriver and then blown off his six-year-old daughter's head with a shotgun. Or the broad who's just burned down her house, except her husband and four kids just happened to be in it.

What are you talking about "you didn't ask to be a cop?" I started being a cop at five. The first Christmas I can remember, under the tree, a fingerprint kit. A goddamn fingerprint kit. And a black-and-white, made out of tin, with your name painted on the hood, "Rusty," and the number of your squad car, "183." I broke it Christmas Day, winding it up, listening to the siren. My God, you had me in uniform when I was ten. All those precinct blasts in "Oakland." Fake ribbons. Fake medals. All the ribbons and medals I was supposed to earn when I grew up. First in the Army, and then on the force. You got me a flasher for my bike. I was eleven years old, and I was arresting every other kid on the block!

[Published by Samuel French]

WHO THEY ARE AND HOW IT IS WITH THEM
by Grace McKeaney

Biz is an ex-con and an ex-boxer who now works as a window wiper. He was imprisoned for small-time racketeering and is on parole. In this piece, he is speaking to his best friend and sidekick, Finny, who is an ex-mental patient in Biz's care until he reorients himself with society.

(*Note: Actor needs to establish the sway of the scaffolding as the wind blows it.*)

BIZ: There's a chip, dent, and bump sale going on right now down at Window City. We should get down there while the sale's going on. We could replace some things, I think. I don't like seconds but figure, how bad can it be? A chip, a dent, a little bump here, a little bump there, here a bump, there a bump . . . who's gonna say something? Let him without a dent, huh? Let him without a dent cast the first one, am I right? 'Cause after all is said and done, you don't need precision, all's you need is fairly decent equipment.

(*The scaffolding begins to sway in the wind.*)

But soon, you know?

(BIZ *takes* FINNY's *squeegee blade, looks at it.*)

I mean, this, for one thing—the rubber on this is going . . . (*Peers at it more closely.*) The rubber on this is *gone*! Fuck and a half, we gotta replace this stuff, man. What have you been wiping with? See, it does not take much. One little slip with a piece of junk like this—one teeny-weeny little false step in the wrong direction. (*Looks down.*)

You get the *Star*? This article in the *Star* says, dig: "This is the second most dangerous profession in the whole fucking world. Because of the element of height added to the element of current air. We're talking about that which is essentially unpredictable. You don't need the earthquake. I mean, baby, call off that tornado. A slight breeze . . . under the wrong conditions . . . And you got . . . *fall time.*

With all that, with this, that, and the other thing, it pays on the whole . . . On the whole, you want relatively sound, relatively safe equipment . . . Perfect, no. A bump here, a dent there, hey, I'm not worried. (*Another blast of wind.*) I'm not worried . . .

So, we'll go down to Window City after and load up. We can make deals! But I say, fuck, get the stuff now and ask later. I say, charge it. I don't carry that kind of cash, do you? I mean if I had that kind of cash, damned if I'd be going down to Window City, man, I'd travel. See the U.S.A. See the world! (*Points down.*) I mean, *there it is*. Buildings! Cars! There! One little shopper meeting another little shopper . . . way . . . down . . . there!

(BIZ *gulps, looks up.*) Clouds! Pretty little clouds!

Treetops! Fresh air current . . . (*The wind drives through.*)

I'm only doing this temporary. You? I have other things in my palm. I went to see somebody who sees things and she saw very clearly I'd be going on a long journey. I said, when's it start? She says, it's already started.

(*Extreme disgust.*) Are you a religious person? I got a question for you: What do you suppose God said under his breath when he saw what he had done—say after the seventh day—say after separating the darkness from the light, the water from the dry land, the forest from the trees, the men from the boys or the girls, the richer from the poorer, the sickness from the health? What do you suppose He said after he realized he'd made so goddamned many *distinctions*?

You know what the first is . . . you know what the world's first most dangerous profession is . . . I think they said . . . just *walking around*.

Finny is an ex-mental patient and Harvard Ph.d. He has had trouble in the past distinguishing the nature of reality from his fantasies. In this monologue, madness is beginning to gradually overtake him again. It is not a furious, volatile descent into insanity. Rather, there is something disquietingly peaceful about his step over the line. This is a brilliant mind at work.

FINNY: I had a dream. I was living in Philadelphia at the time. My body was doing its business in Philadelphia. I had a job as a window wiper in one of the banks downtown. Squeegee-squeegee, all day long. I was an anonymous window wiper in Philadelphia at one time or that is what I recollect. There was a comfort in it. Just me, the glass, the dirt of ages. We knew where we stood, or so it seemed to me. I grew complacent.

I lived in three rooms. I lived out of three rooms. I ate my simple dinner over a sink. I cleaned my solitary space each night. It was a matter of choice. First the rugs, beat, beat, beat. Then the tiles, wipe, wipe, wipe, wipe. I took great care with the dusting of objects. Last of all, I'd take a broom and pan and give the whole flat surface a thorough going-over. Under the couch I'd go, under the bed, the desk. Nothing stopped me. I was indomitable. And when I was done, the process was complete, I'd take the precious fruits of my labors, a pound, two pounds of debris, and coolly toss the sum out the back door, over the low wall into the backyard of a dweller I had never met. This was my nightly procedure. I lived on the second floor. No one was ever looking.

One night, having completed the procedure, imaging nothing, desiring nothing, having nothing whatever to do in its stead, I *repeated* the procedure from beginning to end. A really thorough going-over ensued. Not only the closets, the doors, and the floors, but the walls were swept. I swept windowsills. I swept appliances. I gathered a harvest of lint from my clothing. To my surprise, to my astonishment: two more pounds of debris were duly collected and eliminated. A vague terror welled within me. Panic eventually set in. More dirt lay hidden. Experience allowed me this conclusion, but the terror was: Would there ever come an end to it? I repeated the procedure: two pounds. I repeated the *exact* procedure: *Four pounds* of debris was gathered. I stood in the center of the room with sweat running from my fingertips.

I shut all the windows. I put more locks on the doors. I sealed cracks securely with bits of paper. Then I sat in the stillness and waited. And the dust fell. In planes. It teamed like rain all around me. As fast as I could cup my hands, they were full of stuff. The world was decomposed in my hall, in my kitchen, in my lap. Dust fell from the spaces between molecules separating. But only I had eyes. I sat for days. Then weeks. Cobwebs covered my eyes like awnings. At each miniscule movement of my body, a cake of dust would fall, would burst in smoky clouds. I fainted several times. Perhaps I only slept. When I woke, I was suffocating. The window was near. A great cloud of dust hovered outside, awaiting entrance.

It *smiled* at me. I had no time to think. I broke the glass with my arms. I broke it with my head. I shattered the glass and fell through the air like a willow leaf.

That day, I broke all the windows in the downtown bank. I went uptown and broke the rest. I battered car windows and revolving doors. I pushed over mailboxes. I ran my car into a wall. I set fire to my apartment building. I lay in the road and tore at the tar with my bare hands. I cut down streetlights with an acetylene torch and dismantled buildings brick by brick.

The odd thing is . . . the true irony is . . .

I've never been to Philadelphia.

[Available at New Dramatists]

ABOUT SALLY
by Ellen McLaughlin

In this monologue, a man in his thirties remembers the premature birth of his daughter, Sally.

MAN: See, the problem was that I knew the sex of the child. It was a girl, and for some reason I just assumed that her name would be Sally. It's funny, there was just no question for me; from the very beginning that was her name. Actually, I never talked to my wife about it. I don't know why. Maybe 'cause I didn't want to give the name up. I don't know. She probably would have gone along with it but—not that it—not that that's—I mean that's kind of immaterial now. So anyway, we had the test to find out if it was a boy or a girl—well, Nancy's a real no-nonsense person, she wanted to know what kind of clothes and things to get and that was just that. (*Laughs.*) I wasn't all that pleased—I mean, I was thrilled, of course, I was, it's just, when I first knew, for *certain,* I guess I was just slightly disappointed. I come from a family of women and at work I'm surrounded by women, and I love women, but you know . . . you know. But the thing was, what started happening was—it was amazing

—I began having these absolutely crystal-clear dreams, which I'd remember when I woke up, and this is very unusual for me. And, I mean, these were mind-blowingly large and in color and wraparound. And in them I was doing things with this fabulous little girl, and I realized that she must be Sally—well, actually, she told me at one point—she taps me on the shoulder as we're sitting on top of the Eiffel Tower watching these flamingos—well, I won't go into *that*—anyway, she just says, "Hey, in case you haven't caught on yet, I'm Sally, twerp." And it was like—(*Slaps his forehead.*) Doi, right, of course. And I look at her, I just marvel at her, I mean the presence of her, my own child. And I mean, it was totally believable. I mean, she wasn't perfect-looking or anything—she had these kind of nerdy narrow shoulders and she was slightly pigeon-toed, like me, and lank hair, like Nancy, but here she was, utterly real. And I'd wake up, having just been with her, and I would roll over and look at Nancy's belly, just stare at it, smiling, 'cause I knew she was in there, biding her time. I was very impatient to meet her, which I've sometimes thought was what caused it, you know, the thought that maybe *I* made her premature. Oh, you know, all the bullshit you do to yourself.

Really the worst thing was that she lived for a whole afternoon. I mean, I actually held her, as much as you can, with those plastic mitts that go into the oxygen tent. Oh Jesus. No, it's not that I wish she hadn't lived those four hours—obviously, you know, I just wish . . . anyway . . . She *was* pigeon-toed, you know . . . although that was the least of her problems. In fact, that gave her a kind of panache, if you ask me.

ABOUT SALLY

She actually opened her eyes and looked at me, late in the afternoon, and the look was so old, so sort of bemused, like "Can you believe this?" and she died ten minutes later, when I left the room.

You know that word "bereft?" I heard it the other day and I thought, yeah, that's it, that's . . . So anyway, that was . . . well, that was Sally.

[Available at New Dramatists]

A NARROW BED
by Ellen McLaughlin

John is a young man in his late teens, early twenties. It is 1967 and he is in Vietnam, speaking his letters home to his wife, Megan. He is near the end of his tour of duty and has seen a lot of action.

JOHN: All this talk about sending Americans to the moon—shit, they already did, lots of us. Vietnam, man. Green cheese.

Fuck the fucking space program—that's tiddlywinks, we're here already.

They bring us here and then they leave, and we're supposed to collect moon heads, moon boots, moon tags, a moon leg or two. And the dust. They don't tell you—it's *red*, we walk around on it—fucking treacherous red moon dust.

Yeah, it looks like earth, that's the thing, it *looks* kind of like earth, so you walk around on it as if it was earth, not moon dust.

But then there's this click every once in a while, a click, and then a long, long silence, while you look at your foot and you can't move it, and then, oh yes, you're spattered out in various pieces, out into space again, astronaut that you are, and you become planets of eye, tooth, toe—

And you circle the earth with all the other eye, tooth, toe planets that used to be friends of yours, and the earth is turning beneath you, there are farmers in fields and cars on the highway, but they don't know and they're too far away to tell—and you couldn't tell them anyway, because you're dead.

Willy is a man in his early forties who has been hospitalized for pancreatitis, brought on by his alcoholism. In this monologue, he picks apart the A and B personality-type theory with a nurse who has been taking care of him.

WILLY: No, no, no, they are far more than conceptual tools—uh, uh—they are very dangerous things indeed. They are little rosaries for people who aren't sick, you can fondle your A and B theory and say, "Oh, I'm not constipated, I don't repress my feelings, I'm not burdened with guilt and fear, ergo I'm not going to die of cancer—I'm too hip to myself to die of cancer. These other fools dying—Oh, they just don't know how to express anger" or whatever it is. Or: "I'm calm, laid-back, reasonable in my ambitions, I'm not orally fixated, ergo I'm not going to die of a heart attack." It's this psychological smugness I'm talking about. I wish we were still in the days when people wore garlic around their necks and walked backward on Wednesdays or whatever to ward off evil—I mean, at least then we were a bit more humble in the face of what we feared the most, what we have no control over. What type do you think I am? On second thought, don't tell me. I'd just as soon not hear it. Gosh, it seems fate doesn't have much of a hand in things, not like the old days. Now, on top of being sick, you have to be embarrassed for being sick at all, now it's just a symptom of how unhip you are. And when I think of the people I know—there are an awful lot of very messed-up people out there while I'm in here, they're walking around—and I mean *deluded*, and they don't even have a head cold, while I'm in here a lot, I really am in a lot of pain right now, did you know that? Oh, yes, of course you know that. You're here to cheer me up, aren't you? How silly of me. (*Laughs.*) I know, I know, I started it. I asked you a few questions, but you *answered them*, didn't you?

You think I'm a B, don't you?

You can see it, can't you? I bet you walk down the lines of the beds in the ward going, "A, B, A, A, B, B, B, A . . ." Oh yes, you do. And you zeroed in on me immediately, as soon as I was admitted, you said to yourself, here's this aging pothead gone to Jack Daniels, maybe once he thought he was a painter or a sculptor or something, but now he's dribbled his little life away being a nice guy who never did much of anything. I knew it. I knew I couldn't get an A over a B—see there?—that's the real insidious thing about all this, isn't it? The *grade system mentality. That's* what's at the bottom of all of this, because you *know* that despite the fact that people have strokes and lose their minds and so forth, that we would all much rather have heart attacks than die hard, horrible, painful cancer deaths. You *know*—hey, don't leave me, O.K.?

I know your name tag says Constance, but do people call you Connie?

Connie?

Could you get me a bottle?

[Available at New Dramatists]

MAKING A KILLING
by John Nassivera

To ensure the success of his new play, Ted, a Broadway playwright, stages his suicide on opening night. Now, after escaping to Vermont, he's beginning to have second thoughts after the scam he, his wife, and his producer have pulled. In this monologue, he confesses his yearning to actually dive off the bridge into the river's blackness.

TED: I don't know. I mean, uh, when I started setting up this whole thing, I wasn't sure. I, uh, thought maybe I just might go ahead. I mean, really jump once I actually got up there. (*Laughs slightly to himself.*) God, the weather was horrible—snow, rain, sleet. There was ice on everything. I climbed up on the guardrails, and I stood there. The wind came down the river and blew the sleet in my face so hard it stung. The lights on the bridge were red for Christmas. I looked down and I could just barely see the river. It must be two, three, three hundred feet down. And it's just black. The red lights reflected off some of the ripples in the surface—they're probably waves, but from up there they're just little flashes of light in the blackness.

You see, the wonderful thing about water at night is that you can't really tell that it's there. I used to swim in an old abandoned quarry at night when I was a kid. We'd dive off a cliff where we knew it was safe, and just feel when we would hit this black something. Then the it would be all around you, and you could actually feel it. You could feel the blackness. You'd get turned around under the water after the dive and you'd have to stop moving and stay perfectly still, so you could feel which way the top of the blackness was. It was a thrill, because you knew the quarry was a hundred feet deep, and if you swam the wrong way you could just keep going and going and it would get colder and colder—that was the only way you knew you were going down instead of up. And then you would feel the pressure all around you, because it was trying to get inside you. Because it wants you. I used to swim down as far as I could until I swore I couldn't hold my breath long enough to get back up.

That night, with the wind coming down the river, just standing there, it felt like you were already in the air. Like you'd already made the dive. It would have felt just like diving into that quarry when I was a kid. I wanted to dive off so much . . . I wanted to be a kid again. Just for those few seconds. Those few seconds before the blackness would come.

[Published by Samuel French]

EVERY MOMENT
by OyamO (Charles F. Gordon)

Two young black men, who are ordinarily employed as messengers in downtown New York City, rehearse for a show/rally that is intended to drum up support for black South African freedom fighters. One of them thinks they should be paid for their music and poetry performance. The other, Ben, an idealist, tries to convince his partner that doing the show for free is in their own best interests. In the following passage Ben tells his partner the story behind why he feels compelled to do the performance.

BEN: It was freezing outside. He stood near the radiator in the outer lobby. He smiled at me; I smiled back. I thought to myself, "He smiles as if he's known me all my life." I put my key in the door and he spoke to me: "Cold enough for you?" I said: "There's cold enough for everyone to get his share." He chuckled at this and beckoned me over to him. I don't know why I went, but somehow I felt compelled to. His eyes were clear and transfixed on something in my eyes. He told me that he had come on a mission from South Africa many years ago. He said he had been sent to America by the Archservant to recruit young men to fight in South Africa. For an instant, and only an instant, I did think this old man was hallucinating, like my grandfather often did before he died. But he continued talking and what he said startled me. He told me that I was one of those who he had been sent to recruit. *He said that he had spoken to my dead father about it.* How did he know my father was dead? He told me that my poetry would become songs of liberation in South Africa. How did he know I wrote poetry? He told me to quit N.Y.U. and finish my university studies after the war for liberation had been won. How did he know I went to New York University? I had never seen this man before in my life. He took my hand in his and with his other hand he touched my forehead, just above and between my eyes. He prayed to the Archservant and asked that I be protected on my journey to South Africa. Then he smiled once more at me before he walked out into the freezing cold night.

The next day I was asked to do a benefit for the Azanian Liberation Support Group. I quit night school even though I'd never heard of them before.

[Available at New Dramatists]

THE BOYS OF WINTER
by John Pielmeier

This play takes place during the Vietnam War.

DOC: Funny thing about this war, sir, is it got us doin' shit we'da never dreamed possible. I hear about this My Lai and now the shit that Bonney pulled and I don't condone it, sir, but we all did it. We all have little My Lai's in the corners of our souls, you as well as me, and this war just pointed 'em out a little more clearly. I mean, you gun down some old women and a bunch of kids there's not much more you can learn about yourself, know what I mean? You stand there wonderin' how the hell he coulda done it and I just thank my lucky stars it wasn't me.

So don't blame *him*, sir. You're the ones taught us how to kill. I mean, if this country gonna fight a war you gotta take responsibilities for the casualties of that war. You don't bring 'em to trial. You don't ignore 'em when they ask for help. You don't not celebrate what they tried to do for their country. You understand what I'm saying? Responsibility has got to be taken! You betrayed us, sir, you and Kennedy and Johnson, General Westmoreland, John Wayne, you

lied to us, you're a bunch of fuckin' old men, you were
jealous 'cause we were too goddamn young!

It's you, sir, you're the ones shoulda been thrown
into a ditch and shot.

MONSOON: I mean, when I was a kid, sir, it was
nigger this nigger that my daddy braggin' about how
he strung up some darky just for lookin' at a white
woman. I mean, I got my Klan membership and everything, and lo and behold I'm over here cryin' my
eyes out and this goddamn black dude's offerin' me his
hanky! I couldn't fuckin' believe it! But that's the
secret, sir, I mean the battlefield's the only one hundred percent pure goddamn democracy we'll ever know.
I mean, them bullets they got *no* prejudice. So here I
am holed up with this brother and we're cryin' together and shittin' together and sleepin' so close I
could feel his breath—I woke up one night and I saw
the moon dancin' on his skin, this part in the throat
right here with his heart beatin' against it, and I swore
if Charlie did anything to that dude I'd tear the
motherfucker's head off. That's the reason for most of
the shit, sir. Your buddy trusts you with his life, some
gook pops him in the head, the next coupla dinks
you see you're gonna send to fuckin' Buddha, no
questions asked, 'cause they ain't worth one beat of
his heart against this place in the throat.

L.B.: Sex and death!

Sex and death. You wanna know the truth, sir, I got
it all figured out.

See here I am two months in-country and all of a once I'm caught in this firefight with my pants down takin' a shit, see, and this brother starts crawlin' up to me with his stomach in his hands—hold on, sir, I got a point to make here I mean, you wanna get to the bottom of this, right?—so I kinda tuck this brother back together and I'm lyin' there waitin' for the duster with my hand up to my wrist inside him and my pants down around my ankles and I'm thinkin', Shit, man, I ain't even been this intimate with Bernice. And all of a once, sir, I start to kinda like it, you know what I mean? I mean, here I am ain't had a woman for months about ready to fuck this guy in the stomach and all of a once I realize that that's what this war's all about. Fuckin' and dyin', fuckin' and dyin', got so you can't tell the difference. I mean, best fucks I ever had was the Quang Tri whores 'cause they had that look in their eye, you know? I mean, we were intercoursin' the whole country, sir, let's face it. Save 'em from communism, bullshit, America just want a little pussy. And the Marines in the field, man, they're ashamed 'cause they're rapin' twelve-year-old girls, humpin' grandmothers, and it's so terrible, man, you can't drag yourself away. The tracers in the night, I never seen anything so beautiful, napalm, white phosphorous, gorgeous, baby. And all of a once it got so you just as soon shoot 'em instead of fuck 'em. Every time you seen a body your heart took a leap cause it wasn't you, man, that was the mind-fuck of it all, you were still *alive*.

That girl that Bonney shot, the first one, the one everyone said was Charlie? He was sleepin' with her, sir. She was his number one whore. He knew the whole family, they treated him like a son. And three days after our mission he walks into the village and blows 'em away. Fuckin' and dyin', sir. He couldn't tell the difference anymore. He was horny for death, sir, and inside his pants he was lovin' every minute of it.

[Available at New Dramatists]

NEW ORDER
by Sheldon Rosen

Jay, who is approaching forty, is trying to explain to his long-time girl friend Ell why things have changed and why he's begun to disintegrate. He has become practically inert in his life.

JAY: I was in Australia, and we got out of one of our sessions early, so I decided to go back to my hotel room and take a little rest. I was lying on the bed with the television on when the telephone rang. I must have dozed off, because I wasn't very clearly focused.

"Jay."

Yes.

"How are you?"

Fine.

"Good. Jay?"

Yes.

"We've been watching you for quite a while now."

You have?

"Yes. I'd like to make you a proposition. We'd like you to come away with us. Give up everything. Friends. Job. Apartment. Everything. And what we can promise you in return is a life of meaningful and interesting activity and being part of something larger than yourself. The only thing is, you have to decide now. If you decide to come with us, then meet us at 349 Glebe Point Road in half an hour."

How did you choose me?

"Someone recommended you."

Who?

"I'd rather not say."

That was basically it. Was I ready to give everything up? Was I ready never to see you again? Was I ready to change my life completely? How could I make a decision like that? I had too many other people to think about. Like you, for example. But I also knew I wasn't really going anywhere. I remembered how unhappy you seemed the night I left. How unhappy I was right at that moment. So I went to 349 Glebe Point Road. It was a bar. Some guys from the convention were there. You see, the whole thing was a joke. But it was too late. In the process of making my decision, something snapped and I knew, joke or otherwise, I couldn't go back to my life the way it was. Unfortunately, I no longer had something new with which to replace my life. I no longer had something to become a part of.

[Available at New Dramatists]

TALL TALES
by Robert Schenkkan

J. T. Wells is a country boy turned land agent for the Great Northern Mining Companies, cheating his own people out of their mineral rights with a gift for gab and a little cash. Feeling a little drunk, a lot of guilt, and very confused by the generosity and love of this woman who has just saved his life not an hour after he swindled her father, he breaks down and confesses who he is and what he really represents.

J. T. WELLS: Will you stop being so goddamn understanding about everything! Goddamn hillbillies! (*Getting hysterical.*) You hungry? Here, take my dinner! You tired? Here, take my bed! Here's my daughter, here's my wife, here's my land! What can we do for you, Mr. J.T.? Make yourself at home, sir! Lord, that's a good story, J.T., Lord that is! Few more yams, J.T.! ?

You're all such goddamn children! Eyes big as saucers. (*Crying.*) I could cut your goddamn hearts out with a rusty razor, but as long as I smiled and told another story you'd just sit there happy as pigs in shit!

Oh Lord, I can't do this no more, I can't do this.

Everything I ever told you, it's all lies. All of it. (*Laughs.*) Your poor old pa, thinking he's slick as goose shit. A dollar an acre! What a joke! Oh, he really got me, he did, burned my ass, your old man! There he is sitting on top of maybe fifteen–twenty thousand tons of coal an acre! Millions of dollars he sold me for a lousy buck! Millions! Oh, he's slick, he is, that hillbilly, probably laughin' himself to sleep, poor dumb son of a bitch!

"I swear, I promise. They be real careful with your land, mister." I seen what they do. Over in Harlan County I seen it once. Oh yes sir, they careful. Careful not to miss a trick. First they come in, cut down all your trees . . . Listen to me, goddamn it! They cut down all your trees for railroad ties or shore timbers, whatever. Then they blast the top soil to get down to the surface veins. They scoop it out, wash it down with water from your creeks. Then they cut into the land, deep, start huntin' those deep veins, digging them out in their deep mines. And all the time they're dumping their tailings, all that crap they can't use, full of poison, wherever they see fit. In your streams, in your wells, in your fields, wherever. And when they finished, after they squeezed out every nickel, they just move on to the next one, leaving your land colder and deader'n that moon up there.

J. T. WELLS: I swore a long time ago I'd get outta these mountains whatever it took, but every time I got close something would get in my way. I knocked around plenty until I finally figured it out, till I finally understood how things work. It was so simple. Everybody got their own "truth," see, which is to say their own collection of *stories*.

Your daddy got a story. That he's the son of pioneers; honorable men who risked their lives to carve out a home outta these mountains. That ain't the truth! He's the son of thieves. Who came here and slaughtered the Indians and took their land.

The people I work for, those Standard Oil people, they aren't any different. They're thieves, too. They'll pay your daddy a dollar an acre and congratulate themselves on their honesty. But they stealin' this land from your daddy sure as his daddy stole it from the Indians! And you think they'll sleep any worse at night than your pa does?

When they come in here and cut those trees down, maybe they'll cut the heart out of that old oak you love so much, and ship it off to New York. And somebody'll cut it into a fine banker's desk and swivel-back chair for Mr. Rockefeller himself. You think when he sits his fat ass down on that polished surface he gonna be thinkin' about some poor hillbilly girl whose heart got broke in the process? You won't be part of his *story*, Mary Anne! And when I finish my job for him, I won't be part of his story, either.

There's your truth!

[Available at New Dramatists]

WHY I DRINK
by John Patrick Shanley

Why I drink. Nerves. My nerves try to talk to me and I shut them up by drinking. I drink so that I won't talk about something important. To keep from feeling because if I feel, I will talk and change the spirit in the room dangerously. I drink to keep apart from other people to be invulnerable to become wholly separated from my spirit to become soulless because my soul is a burden to me. I drink because I want to be an animal and love no one and create nothing. A friend once said to me, drink in hand: I drink because it is the only thing that isn't painful. Being drunk is sad sweet partial. Pieces of me become left out. All the moving and shaking pieces. They become invisible. And when they become invisible they also get very powerful and finally take over like a mindless force which is really the most intelligent part of me. It knows what I really want. It rises up, blind, amoral, absolutely true and therefore beautiful and terrifying, and steals me like a boy steals a car. I act with the purity of a character in a dream. I am alone in the night and people who see me and talk to me recognize that I am a natural force unjudgable and strangely attractive because of my irresistible nature. Women take for granted that I will love them physically only because I am only physical.

Men make room for me, exclude me from their quarrels and anger. Animals know that I am one of them. I am hungry. I look for food. I eat in restaurants off the ground. I eat the leaves from the trees. Truly a wild man. Taking no pleasure in being wild but only in being. I stand by a barrel fire with strangers in a trainyard. The flames rush up in yellow sheets. A man strikes the barrel side. Bucketfuls of sparks glitter in all our eyes. All the men I stand with are drunk. The fire holds us all, comforts us all. We are happy for it to hold us, for we think of nothing and take comfort in that. Our faces are haggard with dead or shining eyes. We care for no one. We have no history. We cannot sin or act or contribute or love, but we can drink and we can watch the flame. Eventually there will be sleep. It is unwanted and afterward everything will be bad.

[Available at New Dramatists]

MY LIFE IN ART
by Victor Steinbach

Clement William Tyrrell is a back-country farmer and ex-marine sergeant. The soul of normalcy, salt of the earth, spitting image of your crotchety, lovable old granddad, he goes to New York to claim some livestock that ran away from his Virginia farm. There, he finds himself in the midst of a bizarre series of events.

CLEMENT:

Dear Sir:

I am addressing you, the American Bar Association of New York, on a matter of the utmost importance relating to a deep personal trauma.

I declare that three years ago on the day before Christmas, namely December 24, a goat that I own and call Billy escaped from my farm in Bushville, Virginia.

For proof of this you can check the December 27, 1981, issue of the *Bushville Star* where I placed an ad with the headline "Goat Disappears." On February 12, 1982, I ran a repeat ad offering a hundred-dollar reward.

Those and other steps that I undertook did not lead to his capture, and so it went until October 1984, when I discovered some leads to his whereabouts from unexpected channels and finally found out where he is.

In connection with this I report that the goat that escaped from my farm three years ago had changed a great deal due to some unclear reasons, and is presently residing in New York, where he works in the Minskoff Theatre in the show *The King and I,* playing the King.

In connection with this I report that the person who is known to many as the actor William Tyrrell is not a person. He is really my escaped goat Billy that ran off from my farm three years ago under circumstances undoubtedly criminal; that is, he unlawfully took possession of the following personal items:

1. 1847 Roger Bros. silver dining set, 46 pieces, valued at $1500.00.

2. Gillette straight-edge shaving razor with ivory handle, valued at $25.00.

3. McIntosh wool tie, dark green, valued at $10.00.

4. Felt hat, grey, unknown make, valued at $5.00.

5. A Purple Heart that goes back with me to the days of Iwo Jima, with my name and serial number engraved.

Total of fifty pieces. The prices on the first four items are as of 1952.

I stress the fact that although I sometimes noticed strange and unexplainable things in my goat's behavior before, when he was on my farm, I in no way consider myself responsible for his unlawful appearance in the show *The King and I*, because I had nothing to do with it; he escaped of his own accord.

[Available at New Dramatists]

THE AWARD
by Jeffrey Sweet

This play is about an adult reverting to adolescence. Lerner, a well-dressed man in his mid-thirties, is discovered holding an award he has just been given. At a moment at which he should be enjoying well-earned recognition for success in the world of grown-ups, Lerner can't help but harken back to a teenage frustration. On the surface, of course, he is denying the hold of the past, but the energy he invests in the denial gives lie to this.

LERNER: Thank you. This is an honor I never dreamed I'd . . . I mean, the Charles Jensen Briggs Award! There are so many people to thank. Professor Herman Krause, who was the first to encourage me. The Leona Fielding Foundation for the funding, because, let's face it, this does cost money. And, of course, my colleagues in the lab—Ira Crutcher, Fred Jory, Anita Pleshowsky, and Andy Kramer. And, of course, I want to . . . Wait a second, did I say Anita Pleshowsky? I'm sorry. I meant Anita Petrakoff. Petrakoff, Pleshowsky—you can see how I might, uh, confuse . . .

(LERNER *tries to remember.*)

Pleshowsky. Anita Pleshowsky . . . Oh, yes. I remember Anita Pleshow—we were in junior high school together. That's right. Mr. Champion's homeroom. Oh, yes, I used to think that Anita was about the neatest person in the world. I would write her notes in social studies. Also in music, English, math, and hygiene. I would have written her notes in gym, but, of course, boys and girls don't do gym together. Though sometimes I would see her and the other girls in Mr. Champion's class running laps around the playground in their blue shorts and tops.

My feelings for Anita Pleshowsky were . . . well, I thought about her, I dreamed about her, I followed her home and peeked through the window of Alma Ferret's school for charm where she took classes every Saturday at ten-thirty. She played very hard to get. If she saw me looking at her, she would look away, or make a face, or stick her tongue out.

And then, one day, Mr. Newman, the school counselor, called me into his office. He said to me, "Morris, um, I realize that you are a young man—a growing young person—and young people your age start to develop. And this development is sometimes awkward, sometimes painful. Sometimes we find ourselves attracted to another young person—a young lady, say— and we try to express our feelings. This is normal, this is natural. But sometimes the young lady in question doesn't feel the same way we do. This is something we must learn to accept. You in particular must learn to accept this because you find yourself in this situation. You know the young lady I'm referring to, Morris. Now, I think it would be best for everyone concerned if you cool it, OK? Do you understand what I mean? You may go back to your class."

I think of this now. I think of Mr. Newman and the red wisps of hair on his knuckles. I think of the blush that I could feel suffusing my young cheeks upon learning that my secret yearnings and communications were not as secret as I had hoped. I think of these things, and I laugh.

For I have gotten over you, Anita Pleshowsky. You were once the object of my fantasies and daydreams, but that was fifteen years ago, and a lot of time has passed. Other women—nicer than you, smarter than you, prettier than you—have favored me with their company, and not one of them ever found cause to stick her tongue out at me.

I am beyond the reach of your cruelty. No, your sadism! I am untouched by it. Unmoved. If you were to phone me now, if you were to dial the number here—area code 212-555-3076—if you were to call and say, "Morris, I am sorry. Morris, I want you. Morris, can you ever forgive me? Morris, please hold me in your arms and let me know the joy of you!" I would hang up. Just try it and see.

That number again is 212-555-3076.

Thank you for this lovely award.

[Available at New Dramatists]

THE MAGIC REALISTS
by Megan Terry

This play pokes fun at the desperation of conservative business people when faced with the attitudes of the flower children at the height of the Sixties. The enterprising spirit of the young outlaw, Don, is seen to be the same as that of a successful businessman.

In this scene Don is essentially answering a job interview. His intent is to get food. He makes no moral judgments about the events of his past, but views them as would a disinterested bystander.

DON: I'd like to've been here sooner—but I been sort of away from the action. You see, they kept feelin' like they have to put me in the cooler. And—well, the last time they stashed me there was on account a—(*Relating the story of his life; matter-of-factly.*)—I killed this here whole family that wouldn't let me drive their Volkswagen bus. Shot the dog, too. Then I tried to drive. But I didn't know how to drive. So I shot the bus. They busted me—but I escaped. I been walkin' a lot. I just won't be locked up no more. Ever since I was a tiny fella, they had me locked up somewheres. Even my old granddad tied me to the clothesline, or to the tree or porch railin', so's I couldn't get run over or anything. I thought maybe I'd be lucky when he kicked off, but they didn't know what to do with me, so they put me in these here places and every time I'd get a little older, they'd stick me in another place. But I got away. Been travelin'. Climb up and down trees—it takes longer that way, and very interesting. I know a lot about bugs and bees and birds now. Been studyin' 'em, firsthand. And I found this terrific woods here. Must be some ways from yer camp here? Know somethin'? You're the first guy I talked to since I sprung myself from the can. . . . They fed us lots a food there. Terrible, but it was lots. I never had a mother. I was a skinny ugly mean little kid and no foster family'd take me; so here I am. Handsome and lovely at last, and too big to be adopted. I'm hungry.

[Published by Samuel French]

THE PEOPLE VS. RANCHMAN
by Megan Terry

This play is a demonstration of how different groups may use a person like Ranchman, who is a convicted rapist, to serve their own ends, either liberal or conservative. In this scene, Ranchman is a character witness on his own behalf.

RANCHMAN: I dig the bags under your eyes, baby. Especially the ones that hang below your shoulders in front there. (*To the audience jury.*) Look, I done good things. Lots of them. For example: One night I'm eating this Chinese food in this Chinese joint. And I'm enjoying my shrimps with spicy onion sauce wrapped in bacon—and this Spanish spade chick comes yelling out of the kitchen, drunk as a skunk—yelling and slamming and falling down and the Chinks from the kitchen is chasing her. And she's waving a meat chopper, and this one skinny little Chink cat wrestles the chopper away from her. I don't know how he done it, his shoulders were only like this. This big. (RANCHMAN *shows how big they were.*) But he gets the killer away from her and gives her a boot in the can right out through the swinging doors. Well, this Spanish spade chick picks herself up, and then she falls down again. She's yelling at this skinny little Chink cat the whole time. And he yells back in Chink at her. (*Yells in Chinese gibberish.*) And then she yells at him—"You fink, you lesbian, you fink, you Chink fink, you cracksucker, you fruit-faced Chink lesbian!" She was just getting comfortable in English at the time. And she's yelling and then she stumbles backward, right into the path of an oncoming bus. I seen it and I run outside and grab her up in one fell swoop, and then I park her on the sidewalk. I saved her life, you see. You see. But she—she's still yelling, "You fink Chink lesbian, you slithead," and she falls down again. But this time she falls on top of me. And she throws up a bushel of what was once chicken chow mein, right down my front. Well, then I started yelling, I couldn't help myself. People react before they think in cases like that. I smashed her face and pushed her right back into the gutter. So you see—my hands ain't exactly clean . . . but they ain't dirty neither. My heart was in the right place till it got vomited on. You have to admit it.

[Published by Samuel French]

BATTERY
by Daniel Therriault

This outburst opens the play. It is morning; Rip enters his appliance-repair shop to start his regular working day and, as usual, lets his apprentice in on the previous evening's events. Rip is an electrician who adapts all people and situations to his own circuit. He is a man filled with the animal joy of being alive, alone in a world of machinery. And this machinery, whether it be flesh or steel, to his mind exists only to be adapted to whatever purpose he desires. Which includes a one-night stand.

RIP: I caught her in my sights at ten o'clock at Fatrack's bar. Took aim at the target, tugged at the trigger, and fired at her with a sloe gin fizz. Shot myself up with a shooter. I made my mark. I was sitting next to her. In like Flynn. She was perfection. Fresh off the assembly line. Her chrome shone. Fire-engine redhead. Not a dent in her fenders. Not a scratch on her doors. And she was soooo young. I'm revving like a tuned engine in neutral, right? I grease her with another sloe gin. I'm talking about a classy chassis. She looks at me dreamy-like and says, "Your eyes are as deep and clear as a Minnesota lake. I want to take off all my clothes and skinny-dip in them."

(*Beat.*)

In my eyes. No clothes. She said that.

(*Beat.*)

Her place. Billows of pillows. She was a natural redhead, know what I mean? Hundred percent Irish, believe me. She sparkled like Waterford crystal. I took out my dipstick to check. She was oozing with oil. We were in park at the head of the strip. I twisted her starter. We kicked over into a steady uphill climb in low. I fit like she was custom made. When the rhythm was right, I threw her into first. We took off like two T-birds dragging down a dirt road. Pumping pistons. Threw it into second. She was in spasms. Forced into third. She blew my circuit. Flipped her over into reverse. We smoked. One greased engine. All jets blasting. To the bone. Busting the sound barrier. My face pressurized into contortions. Two gees, five gees, nine gees. We began fishtailing. Her hips double-jointed. A spiritual experience. The Ascension. The Second Coming. Tongues of fire. The finish line. The flag went down. First place. I grabbed the trophy.

(*Calming.*)

Afterward I cooled my jets. She purred in idle. Even smelt like burnt rubber. She was stuttering and mumbling, trying to form the words "thank you," but her lips were too spent. I said, "Hey, baby, you deserved it." And disappeared. Her name? Who cares what her name was? But she'll remember my name till she dies. Rip. 'Cause I ripped her to pieces. Aces.

[Published by Broadway Play Publishing]

FLOOR ABOVE THE ROOF
by Daniel Therriault

Like the rest of the characters in this drama, Jay, working as a shipping clerk in Manhattan, fights the deadening brutality of manual labor. As other workers combat this condition in their own way, Jay takes refuge in his daughter. Propelled by the anticipation of seeing his little girl this evening after being separated for so long, he does not need to consciously reach for a poetic articulation, but rather his expression flows quite naturally and emerges out of distinct necessity. For if he cannot have the actual hug of his baby to rescue him from the harshness of his daily life, then he will hold onto the embrace of her memory and relish the kiss of his own imagination.

JAY: I got to ask you a favor, El-man. A friend was going to drive me to Kennedy tonight, but his car broke down. My wife and kid're on a plane from Trinidad. I have the money to support them now. You have to see my daughter, man. An island princess, truly. She was three so now she's got to be four. At two she was in the ocean with a blown-up inner tube riding the waves like a cork. And before I left she could count to ten and the ABC's. No lie. My wife fixes her hair in these little rolls with pink ribbons. She looks kind of funny but cute. When this job gets me down and I can't take it anymore, I make my mind far away and think of my little girl. I remember when she was born. I was there with the birthing. So easy, the delivery. Only seven pushes my wife had. And the baby came with no crying. The doctor put her on my wife's stomach and the baby smiled at me. Gums. No crying. Smiling right at me.

(*Beat.*)

She's going to be raised American. Trinidad'll always have a claim on me and the island'll be in her blood and that blood passed on, but she'll be of this island. Manhattan. And that's good.

(*Beat.*)

Work'll be so much easier now. She'll be my reward when I go home. My girl's so lovely, man. Her face is perfectly symmetric. Big, round cheeks sculpted out of black clay. Her nose chiseled. Her ears flawless. And her eyes like the sea at night. Beautifully black against white sand. Big and deep. Life breathing under the surface. Her eyes sparkle like moonbeams on the waves. My baby's eyes. Moon on the Caribbean. The most beautiful in Trinidad. In the Islands. In the world. In the universe, man!

[*Beat.*]

Will you drive me to the airport?

[Published by Broadway Play Publishing]

THE WHITE DEATH
by Daniel Therriault

Sometimes the small have the biggest dreams and the weak, the strongest. This is not the case with Kimo. Though both small and weak, he only dreams to be what he already is, or is supposed to be: boss of his own place. Kimo owns and tends a rundown bar built on the rim of an active volcano in Hawaii. He confesses his desire for beauty and power to a priest who is drinking at the bar. For Kimo, wishing to rule his own bar is like wishing to rule the world.

KIMO: I always like get one class place. But I make one big mistake from the start. I never get no rules. This place complete chaos. Now I gotta serve criminals, prostitutes, and tourists. Even if I get rules, nobody'd listen to me.

(*Beat.*)

But I still get dreams, eh. Sometimes I think like this place is one first-class restaurant. But jus' gourmet Filipino food. Filipino food, it the best in the world. Spicy beef with almonds in the peanut sauce. Ooh, boy, the best. The backroom over there, that the kitchen. All real good, modern appliances. I stay cooking all the food back there. I'm good cook, you know. And when I become one big success, I can teach one young kid for raise him in my style and how for make good like me. Then I can work behind the bar, make up all the drinks. Jus' me, I the only one that know the secret recipe how for make them up. I serve them in long-stem, crystal snifters. Call the drinks Kimo Specials. Nobody can get enough of them. I make the whole bar look like the Philippines. Get like jungle everywhere. Thick green carpet, lotsa flowers, trees, hapu'u. Lace drapes. Chandeliers. Son of a gun. The maitre d', he dress up in one white tuxedo. And the Filipino waitresses all in those brocade sarongs and transparent silk blouses. Boy. And they no walk, they glide, like some kinda breeze. Not a lot of tables, jus' choice ones. All private. Nice, polished koa wood and each chair one tiny little throne. Reservations months in advance. And somebody say something stupid I no like, I jus' tell my bouncers, eh, throw him out, jus' like that. And they do. No tourists. Jus' good people. Locals. Important people come all the way from Honolulu for eat in Kimo's Restaurant. Then I can get respect. Hold my head up. Then I can be one big shot.

Kanaka is a full-blooded Hawaiian living in Hawaii. His basic actions are simple reactions. Reacting to a diseased white society, he develops a skin condition; reacting to racism against him, he becomes a racist; reacting to a white god, he becomes an atheist; reacting to the death of his people, he becomes a murderer. Earlier in the play, he has castrated and then stabbed to death a white tourist. He now brags to a priest in a bar about how he covered up the murder. To Kanaka, killing a tourist is not much different than killing a wild pig, except that killing a boar is more exciting.

KANAKA: Me, I allergic to everything. Alcohol. Cigarettes. Haoles. Before the haoles come, there was no disease. But the haoles come bring their white death. Now everything infection. Not that many full-blooded Hawaiians left. Everything die.

(*Beat.*)

Some guys, they murder with their mind. Put one bullet through the brain. Not me. I kill with my heart. More messy. But I gotta believe in what I do.

(*Beat.*)

Me, I figure I fool everybody. I put the dead body inside the bag, then throw the haole into the back of my pickup truck. I drive to the garbage dump. I could get rid of him inside the compactor, but no, I get more better idea. I wait in the dark for the wild boar for come. I know she come to the dump at night. And then I hear one. Bugger come real slow, yeah. Sniff out for humans. But she no smell me. Bugger come near. I make my move. The pig scared, squeal, run. I jump on her back. Pull out my knife. Cut her neck. Ooh, the bugger let out one big, wet groan. I grab the tusk. Pull the neck back. Snap. Limp. Make.

(*Beat.*)

The moon bright. I cut out one tusk. Take the body out from the bag. In the moonlight I stick the tusk into the pukas the knife wen make in the haole. I go back to Kilauea. Shove him down the throat of the volcano.

Feed him to the crater. The haole like it here so bad, he can stay for good. This not his island.

Glossary: *make* [makay]: dead
         puka [pookah]: hole

Kanaka is not allowed to sleep with Kitty, the local prostitute. This confession to a priest in a bar (a confession that never asks for forgiveness) is about trying to attain the unattainable, in this case, human intimacy. When simple touch is denied, violence is near, and pure bliss can be a finger pressed to a lip.

KANAKA: When I come to town, that's when I like get everything I no can have. Like Kitty. I want her 'cause I no can have her.

(*Beat.*)

I never can get no woman. Not even one prostitute. Nobody like touch me. Nobody. Sometimes me, I get this feeling deep inside of me and jus' like for explode. Like one volcano. Like last night. My skin crawl then I bust out. I think maybe if somebody jus' touch me once in a while, I'd be all right. You know? When I go touch Kitty, she yells and moves away. But when I hit her, she stay still. She no let me hug her, but she let me hit her. So I hit her for touch her. She no like me hit her in the face, so I try not to. But if somebody jus' let me touch them, eh, I no try to hit Kitty. Maybe.

(*Beat.*)

I get this one dream about Kitty, always stay the same. Over and over again. I know what's gonna happen. It's Kitty. She walks up to me real slow. Then puts one finger on my lip, and rubs, back and forth. So soft. Like nobody I ever know. Then last night. In real life. She wen touch me. No kidding. Jus' like that. In this bar. I thought dreams was just dreams. You know, the thing that never comes true. But last night, my dream come true. Kitty wen walk up to me and touch my lip like that. Jus' like my dream.

[Published by Broadway Play Publishing]

FENCES
by August Wilson

Troy Maxson is fifty-three years old. He is a large man with thick, heavy hands. Together with his blackness, his largeness informs his sensibilities and the choices he has made in his life.

In the first monologue, Troy tells his oldest son, Lyons, what his father was like and why he decided to leave home and go out into the world at age fourteen.

TROY: Yeah . . . my daddy was something else. Just as evil as he could be. My mama couldn't stand him. Couldn't stand that evilness. She run off when I was about eight. She sneaked off one night after he had gone to sleep. Told me she was coming back for me. I ain't never seen her no more. All his women run off and left him. He wasn't no good for nobody.

When my turn came to head out, I was fourteen and got to sniffing around Joe Canewell's daughter. We be sneaking off into the woods and things. Had us an old mule we called Greyboy. My daddy sent me to do some plowing and I tied up Greyboy and went to fooling around with Joe Canewell's daughter. We done found us a nice spot . . . got real cozy with each other.

She about thirteen and we done figured we was grown anyway . . . so we down there enjoying ourselves . . . ain't thinking nothing. We didn't know Greyboy had got loose and wandered back to the house and my daddy was looking for us. We down there by the creek enjoying ourselves when my daddy come up on us. Surprised us. Had him them leather straps of the mule and commenced to whupping me like there was no tomorrow. I jumped up mad and embarrassed. I was scared of my daddy. When he commenced to whupping on me . . . quite naturally I run to get out of the way. (*Pause.*) Now, I thought he was mad 'cause I ain't done my work. But I see where he was chasing me off so he could have the gal for himself. When I seen what the matter of it was, I lost all fear of my daddy. Right there is where I became a man . . . at fourteen years of age. (*Pause.*) I ain't knowed what was in the gal's mind except that she was probably scared of him too. But that's when I grew up. Now it was my turn to run him off. I picked up the same reins that he had used on me . . . that he done dropped to have a go at the gal. Now, I ain't stopped to think about what I was doing. If I stopped to think about it I don't think I could have done it. I picked up them reins and commenced to whupping on him. The gal jumped up and ran off . . . and when my daddy turned to face me I could see why the devil had never come to get him . . . 'cause he was the devil himself. I don't know what happened. When I woke up I was laying there by the creek. I thought I was blind. I couldn't see nothing. Both my eyes were swollen shut, and I layed there and cried. I didn't know what I was gonna do. The only thing I knew was that the time had come for me to leave my daddy's house. And right then the world suddenly got big. And it was a long time before I could cut it down to where I could handle it.

In this second monologue, Troy, a robust, life-loving man, tells the story of how he wrestled with Death and won.

TROY: I looked up one day and Death was marching straight at me. Like soldiers on parade! The army of Death marching straight at me. The middle of July 1941. It got real cold just like it be winter. It seem like Death himself reached out and touched me on the shoulder. He touch me just like I touch you. I got cold as ice and Death standing there grinning at me.

I say, What you want, Mr. Death? You be wanting me? You done brought your army to be getting me. I looked him dead in the eye. I wasn't fearing nothing. I was ready to tangle. Just like I'm ready to tangle now. The Bible say be ever vigilant. That's why I don't get but so drunk. I got to keep watch.

Death, he ain't said nothing. He just stared at me. I looked him dead in the eye and said, You be wanting me, Mr. Death? He had him a thousand men to do his bidding and he wasn't gonna get a thousand and one. Not then! Hell, I wasn't but thirty-seven. (*Pause.*) Death standing there staring at me . . . carrying that sickle in his hand. Finally, he say, "You want bound over for another year?" See, just like that . . . "You want bound over for another year?" I told him, Bound over hell! I know you ain't been following me up and down the roads these many years to ask me if I want bound over for another year. I told him, Let's settle this now! If you want me, come on and take me.

It seem like he kinda fell back when I said that, and all the cold went out of me. I reached down and grabbed the sickle and threw it just as far as I could throw it, and me and him commenced to wrestling.

We wrestled for three days and three nights. I can't say where I found the strength from. Every time it seemed like he was gonna get the best of me, I'd reach down way deep inside of me and find the strength to do him one better.

I ain't making up nothing. I'm telling you the facts of what happened. I wrestled with Death for three days and three nights and I'm standing here to tell you about it. (*Pause.*) All right. At the end of the third night we done weakened each other to where both of us could hardly move. Death stood up, throwed on his robe—he had him a white robe with a hood on it. He throwed on that robe and went off to look for his sickle. Say, "I'll be back." Just like that. "I'll be back." I told him, say, I'll be here. I'll be waiting for you. But you gonna have to find me! I wasn't no fool. I wasn't going looking for him. Death ain't nothing to play with. And I know he's gonna get me. I know I got to join his army . . . his camp followers. You can't help that. Death is a natural part of life. But as long as I keep my strength and see him coming . . . as long as I keep up my vigilence . . . he's gonna have to fight to get me. I'm gonna die with my boots on . . . as they say. I don't mind dying . . . 'cause when he carry me across on the other side I'm gonna get to see my mama. The only thing I want is for him to respect me.

That's all. I ain't afraid of dying. Sometime I feel like my whole life happen just to prepare me for that one last battle. That's when you find out what kind of man you are. That's the one they write down in the Book of Life. And they gonna write down that Troy Maxson was a battling sonofabitch who almost retired death! That's what they gonna write.

[Published by New American Library]

MA RAINEY'S BLACK BOTTOM
by August Wilson

The setting for this play is Chicago, 1927. Toledo is
the piano player in Ma Rainey's band. He is in control
of his instrument, yet realizes and understands that its
limitations are an extension of him. He is self-taught
and the only member of the group who can read. As
this monologue shows, he misapplies his knowledge,
though he is quick to penetrate to the core of a situation and his insights are thought-provoking.

TOLEDO: Now, I'm gonna show you how this goes
. . . where you just a leftover from history. Everybody
come from different places in Africa, right? Come
from different tribes and things. Soonawhile they began to make one big stew. You had the carrots, the
peas, the potatoes, and whatnot over here. And over
there you had the meat, the nuts, the okra, corn . . .
and then you mix it up and let it cook right through to
get the flavors flowing together . . . then you got one
thing. You got a stew.

Now you take and eat the stew. You take and make
your history with that stew. All right. Now it's over.
Your history's over and you done ate the stew. But

you look around and you see some carrots over here, some potatoes over there. That stew's still there. You done made your history and it's still there. You can't eat it all. So what you got? You got some leftovers. That's what it is. You got leftovers and you can't do nothing with it. You already making you another history . . . cooking you another meal, and you don't need them leftovers no more. What to do?

See, we's the leftovers. The colored man is the leftovers. Now, what's the colored man gonna do with himself? That's what we waiting to find out. But first we gotta know we the leftovers. Now, who knows that? You find me a nigger that knows that and I'll turn any whichaway you want me to. I'll bend over for you. You ain't gonna find that. And that's the white man. The white man knows you just a leftover. 'Cause he the one who done the eating and he know what he done ate. But we don't know that we been took and made history out of. Done went and filled the white man's belly and now he's full and tired and wants you to get out the way and let him be by himself. Now, I know what I'm talking about. And if you wanna find out, you just ask Mr. Irvin what he had for supper yesterday. And if he's an honest white man—which is asking a whole heap of a lot—he'll tell you he done ate your black ass and if you please I'm full up with you . . . so go on and get off the plate and let me eat something else.

Levee is a trumpet player in his early thirties. He is younger than the other men in the band. He is rakish and bright, and is somewhat of a buffoon. But his is an intelligent buffoonery. This monologue is Levee's response to the other men in the band, who have been riding him about how he acts around the white man.

LEVEE: I was eight years old when I watched a gang of white mens come into my daddy's house to do with my mama any way they wanted.

(*Pause.*)

We was living in Jefferson County, about eighty miles outside of Natchez. My daddy's name was Memphis—Memphis Lee Green—had him near fifty acres of good farming land. I talking about good land! Grow anything you want! He done gone off of shares and bought this land from Mr. Hallie's widow woman after he done passed on. Folks called him an uppity nigger 'cause he done saved and borrowed to where he could buy this land and be independent.

(*Pause.*)

It was coming on planting time and my daddy went into Natchez to get some seed and fertilizer. Called me, say, "Levee, you the man of the house now. Take care of your mama while I'm gone." I wasn't but a little boy, eight years old.

(*Pause.*)

My mama was frying up some chicken when them mens come in that house. Must have been eight or nine of them. She standing there frying chicken and them mens come and took hold of her just like you take hold of a mule and make him do what you want.

(*Pause.*)

There was my mama with a gang of white mens. She tried to fight them off, but I could see where it wasn't gonna do her any good. I didn't know what they were doing to her . . . but I figured whatever it was they may as well do to me too. My daddy had a knife that he kept around there for hunting and working and whatnot. I knew where he kept it and I went and got it. I'm gonna show you how spooked up I was by the white man. I tried my damndest to cut one of them's throat! I hit him on the shoulder with it. He reached back and grabbed hold of that knife and whacked me across the chest with it.

(LEVEE *raises his shirt to show a long ugly scar.*)

That's what made them stop. They was scared I was gonna bleed to death. My mama wrapped a sheet around me and carried me two miles down to the Furlow place and they drove me to Doc Albans. He was waiting on a calf to be born, and say he ain't have time to see me. They carried me up to Miss Etta, the midwife, and she fixed me up.

My daddy came back and acted like he done accepted the facts of what happened. But he got the names of them mens from mama. He found out who they was and then we announced we was moving out of that county. Said good-bye to everybody . . . all the neighbors. My daddy went and smiled in the face of one of them crackers who had been with my mama. Smiled in his face and sold him our land. We moved over with relations in Caldwell. He got us settled in and then he took off one day. I ain't never seen him since. He sneaked back, hiding up in the woods, laying to get them eight or nine men.

(*Pause.*)

He got four of them before they got him. They

tracked him down in the woods. Caught up with him and hung him and set him afire.

(*Pause.*)

My daddy wasn't spooked up by the white man. No sir! And that taught me how to handle them. I seen my daddy go up and grin in this cracker's face . . . smile in his face and sell him his land. All the while he's planning how he's gonna get him and what he's gonna do to him. That taught me how to handle them. So you all just back up and leave Levee alone about the white man. I can smile and say yes sir to whoever I please. I got time coming to me. You all just leave Levee alone about the white man.

[Published by New American Library]

RIMERS OF ELDRITCH
by Lanford Wilson

Skelly is the town lowlife: a Peeping Tom who has been caught having unnatural relations with a farm animal. He wanders about Eldritch, a small former mining town in the Midwest, talking to whomever will listen. In this case, his audience is a stray dog.

SKELLY: And we done it in the old man's woodshed. Oh, sure. I sneaks back the very same night and we done it out in the woodshed there. Everything smelling of hickory and cedar for their fancy fireplaces. Oh, yeah. And, oh, how she did squirm! Oh, Lord. Saying to me, "Oh, I love you. Oh, I love you, oh, really I do, Skelly." Oh shit.

(*Coughs.*)

Till I thought she was gonna croak. Oh, Lord. Never let on she even knew me. Sashay around town with her big hats. Glenna Ann. Pretty girl. Oh, yeah. No girl in town so pretty. Then or now. None in between. How she did claw and bite. No bigger than a mite. Hound. Where'd you go? Don't you bury that. You eat that now. That's good. You are good. Old Man Reiley moved off; she moved off, whole family, lock stock and petticoat. Mines give out, off they git. How she did squirm. Oh, I love you so much. Oh, sure. Pretty girl too. Right in the wood house the very night her old man chased me off with a crowbar. And we sat up against the wall there, playing in the shavings on the floor. Till morning, near. Sure. All blue. The bluest blue in the morning. Blue light on her gown there. Sticking her feet into the shavings—digging. Holding hands petting. Where's that teakettle, huh? Where'd it go? Make some sassafras. Yeah, wouldn't eat it if I gave it to you, would you. Don't know what's good, do you? Beautiful tits; no tits like that when or since. I guess you know Peck Johnson fairly beat the shit out of that girl his last night. Whipped her good. Never seen anything like it. Thought she was dead. Patsy. Little whore she is, too. Thought he nearly killed her. The old lady standing there with her teeth clenched watching, white as a ghost . . . mad as the devil. Good! I say good! Whatever she done, I say good! She deserved it, little whore. Here, you whore. Go on with you! get on out with you. Filthy brother: whole family right along brother and sister both. Beat her till she nearly bled. Thought he was gonna kill her. People don't care! What kind of things goes on. What kind of devilment. Where'd you go to? Hound? What-are-you-not eating? If you was tame you could come out and sit on the street. Catch a rabbit, huh? You scared of rabbits? Are you? That's a good girl. You're okay. Bluest blue you ever saw in the daytime. Cold too and her in a nightgown! run right off of the house when I called up and off we went.

(*Laughs.*)

Oh, boy, Arms is no good. Can't lift 'em even over

my head. Look a there. Oh, boy. Red thing over her nightgown there. Barefoot. Grass sticking to her feet; fresh cut lawns with their lackeys there, mowing and clipping and futzing. Barefoot. Right across the dew and all.

That crippled girl, Jackson, she's got her left shorter, one than the other. Cries. You never saw anything like it. Dances around her room in the window curtains, all lace, wrapped around her whooping, dancing around like a banshee. Oh, he's all right. Tell him I said he's all right. Well, I guess he knows that. No, he don't know it, now, there! Better his no-good brother everybody yelling about; doing it by hand. Hitting girls around. People don't care! They don't see. What. What they want to think they think; what they don't they don't. They don't care anyway; what kind of devilment. What goes on. Her old man, old man Reiley; never did know. No, no. Never did know. I weren't the only one either you can bet. Get some water boiling; make some sassafras; good for the stomach. Cedar. All in the air. Bluest blue in the air. Hickory and cedar cedar cedar cedar cedar in the air. Sang.

(*Laughs.*)

All manner of songs there. Soft so's it wouldn't carry to the lackey's house there. Carrying on, scratching, biting, thought she was gonna croak. Oh, really, Oh, I love you so!

(*Laughs.*)

Pretty girl. Beautiful tits. Beautiful tits. Oh, yes. Oh, sure.

[Published by Hill & Wang]

SERENADING LOUIE
by Lanford Wilson

Alex is in his mid-thirties. Fast becoming a public hero, he's boyish, entertaining, and shrewd. At this moment in the play, however, his marriage is disintegrating and he's faced with a decision to move out of his law practice and into public office. Most of the principles Alex has lived by are coming in for scrutiny as the life he has known dissolves.

ALEX: Jesus, God, you add it all up and I don't understand any of it! The farthest star is several billion light-years away on the edge of the universe—beyond which is nothing, Einstein tells us. Not even cold, empty space. Nothing. Tricky. Now, what is that supposed to mean to me? I have to assume that the Earth and her people might at any moment jump its track and catapult us cold and wet—frosty—into a neighboring solar system—and how stupid, preoccupied, and foolish we'll look. Some embarrassingly superior being will frown questioningly and say, "What do you make of all these facts you present me with?" And we'll say, well, we're working on it. Give us another week. "You mean there are people who are hungry and cold and ten percent of your population controls ninety percent of your food and blankets?" Well, we're working on it. But we're not. We'll do anything except admit that what we've got here is not just a simple problem of distribution. But recently I read a report from the good old government—why I want to be a part of that, I'll never know—that said we (meaning man) have discovered (meaning America, probably) have discovered just about all there is to know. The mind of man has encompassed most all knowledge, and from now on—however far that may be—we will just be in the process of refinement. That's our future. Sandpapering. Where is the man who wrote that living? When is he living? How would that asshole address himself to the complexity of the human being? To, for instance, that horrible moment when I feel I myself just might, one of these deranged and silvery mornings, become that monster you read about who slays his family and himself or fifteen strangers holed up in a tower somewhere . . . come foaming into the breakfast table with your tie awry and your hair uncombed. Moments all the worse because they are recurrent at the most unguarded times when that prospect, however hideous, is very real. In the middle of culminating a particularly successful business deal or relaxing on the beach in the clean salt air, you can still feel it way down deep in your nature somewhere. "Well, tonight, God help me, I may just run completely amok with a meat cleaver."

[Published by Hill and Wang]

RED LETTER DAYS
by Dick D. Zigun

This is a monologue for a man or woman playing a pagan spirit like Ariel or Puck with an ethical standard deviant from those held by warm-blooded humans. On Halloween the dead stand up in their graves and tell stories they have been making up since the midnight of last year's Halloween. The storyteller might think the theft of a newborn child funny and reward the gesture by turning someone into a stone or a tree for nine hundred years.

Ghost Story with Jack O'Lantern

VOICE: Dingdong. I opened the door.

Trick or treat. It was a ghost with an empty sack. I gave the ghost a bag of M&M's. I closed the door.

Dingdong. I opened the door. Trick or treat. It was the same ghost, the same sack. I gave the ghost a quarter. I closed the door.

Dingdong. I opened the door. Trick or treat. Same ghost. I gave the ghost a dozen Mars bars and a couple of dollars. I closed the door.

Dingdong. I opened the door. Trick or treat. I gave the ghost a six pack of beer, my wristwatch, two rings, and my wallet. I closed the door.

Dingdong.

Dingdong.

Dingdong—dingdong—dingdong—dingdong—ding—dong.

I opened the door. Trick or treat. I looked hard at the ghost. Same ghost. Same sack. I gave the ghost my three-month-old son. I closed the door.

Dingdong. A witch opened her door. Trick or treat. It was the ghost with the child in the sack. The witch treated the ghost to a bottle of dragon's breath in exchange for the child. The witch closed the door.

Dingdong. The witch wasn't home. The boy opened the door. He was now five years old. Trick or treat. It was a skeleton selling magazine subscriptions. The boy closed the door.

Dingdong. The witch wasn't home. The lad opened the door. He was now twelve years old. Trick or treat. It was a werewolf wanting to borrow a cup of sugar. The lad closed the door.

Dingdong. The witch wasn't home. The young man opened the door. He was now nineteen years old. Trick or treat. It was a voice on the wind. The young man stepped out into the forest. He left the witch's door open.

Dingdong. The door opened by itself. Trick or treat. It was my son. He smiled. He was tall. He was handsome. He had eyes like a cat. I closed the door. I locked the door. I closed the curtains. I turned off the lights.

Dingdong. I opened the door. Those eyes. My son

gave me an apple. I took a bite. I fell asleep for ten days. I dreamed about my mother and the doctor and the horses and the farm and the night and noises and sounds that you hear in the night.

I opened my eyes. My son gave me a blanket. It was snowing. The door was open. My son gave me another blanket. It snowed harder. My son gave me a third blanket. It snowed like a blizzard. He went out into the forest for firewood. I closed the door.

Dingdong.

Dingdong—dingdong.

I stay in bed dreaming about my mother and the farm and the sounds that you hear in the night.

Dingdong.

I stay in bed under the blankets. I won't open the door.

Dingdong.

I won't open the door.

[Available at New Dramatists]

Appendices

Biographies of Playwrights

Robert Anderson
Plays: *Tea and Sympathy, I Never Sang for My Father, You Know I Can't Hear You When The Water's Running, Solitaire/Double Solitaire.*
Screenplays: *The Nun's Story, The Sand Pebbles.*
Novels: *After, Getting Up and Going Home.*
Past President, Dramatists Guild and New Dramatists.
Theatre Hall of Fame, 1981.
Contact: Mitch Douglas, I.C.M., 40 W. 57th St., New York, NY 10019

Arthur Carter
Plays: *The Number, High Fidelity, The Locked Room.*
Play and Screenplay: *Operation Madball.* Contract writer at Columbia Pictures.
Contact: Arthur Carter, 276 Gano St. (rear), Providence, RI 02906, or Tanya Chasman, Jack Rose Agency, 6430 Sunset Blvd. (Suite 1203), Hollywood, CA 90028

Edward M. Cohen
Plays: *Cakes with the Wine, The Complaint Department Closes at Five.*
Novel: *$250,000* (Putnam). Stories have appeared in *Evergreen Review* and *Carleton Miscellany.*

Associate Director of New York's Jewish Repertory
Theatre.
Contact: Edward M. Cohen, 949 West End Ave., New
York, NY 10025

Paul D'Andrea

Plays: *The Trouble with Europe, Bully, A Full Length
Portrait of America,* with John Klein, cowrote *The
Einstein Project.*
Awards: Fulbright, Rockefeller, Bush, McKnight and
Jerome Fellowships, 2 FDG/CBS Awards, ATL Great
American Play Prize.
Contact: George Lane, William Morris Agency, 1350
Ave. of the Americas, New York, NY 10019

Allen Davis III

Plays: *Where the Green Bananas Grow, The Head of
Hair, The Rag Doll, Bull Fight Cow, Montezuma's
Revenge, Don't Breathe on the Job.* He has published
two children's plays with Samuel French.
Awards: NEA, CAPS, fellowships from eight art colo-
nies. Presently director of the Playwrights Workshop,
Puerto Rican Travelling Theatre.
Contact: Allen Davis III, 484 W. 43rd St. Apt. 20-F,
New York, NY 10036

Russell Davis

Plays: *The Last Good Moment of Lilly Baker, The
Day of the Picnic, The Further Adventures of Sally,
Sally's Gone, She Left Her Name.*
Awards: NEA, McKnight, N.Y. Foundation for the
Arts, Tennessee Arts Commission, N.Y. State Council
on the Arts.
Contact: Joyce Ketay, 334 W. 89th St., New York,
NY 10024

Richard Dresser

Plays: *Better Days, The Hit Parade, At Home, Splitsville, Road to Ruin, Alone at the Beach, The Downside. Bait and Switch* and *Amnesia* have both been workshopped at the Eugene O'Neill National Playwrights Conference. Contact: Jeanine Edmunds, 230 W. 55th St., 29-D, New York, NY 10019

Rosalyn Drexler

Plays: *Home Movies, The Writer's Opera, Dear, The Line of Least Existence, Theatre Experiments, Transients Welcome, The Mandrake, Starburn, Delicate Feelings, The Investigation, Hot Buttered Roll, Skywriting, The Bed Was Full,* etc.
Fiction: Seven novels. *Dear* was first published as a short story in the *Paris Review.*
Other: Three museum shows in 1987: Gray Gallery, N.Y.U.; Greenville County Museum of Art, N.C.; Univ. of Iowa Museum of Art, Iowa.
Awards: Two Obies, Guggenheim, Emmy, three Rockefellers, CAPS grant, MacDowell Fellow, Yaddo Fellow, *Paris Review* Humor Prize, etc.
Contact: Fifi Oscard Associates, Inc., 19 W. 44th St., New York, NY 10036

Gus Edwards

Plays: *The Offering, Weep Not for Me, Louie and Ophelia.*
Awards: NEA, Rockefeller.
Contact: Susan Schulman Literary Agency, 454 W. 45th St., New York, NY 10036

Mary Gallagher

Plays: *Father Dreams, Buddies, Dog Eat Dog, Chocolate Cake, Little Bird, How to Say Goodbye.*

Awards: NEA, Rockefeller, Guggenheim.

Screenplay: Co-author with Ara Watson of *Nobody's Child*, a multiple award-winning TV movie.

Contact: Bret Adams, Ltd., 448 W. 44th St., New York, NY 10036

Anthony Giardina

Plays: *Living at Home, The Child, Scenes from La Vie de Boheme, Jay, Discovered.*

Novels: *Men With Debts, A Boy's Pretensions.*

Awards: CAPS, MA Artists Foundation.

Contact: Anthony Giardina, 55 South St., Northampton, MA 01060

Jack Gilhooley

Plays: *Shirley Basin, The Brixton Recovery, The Time Trial, Spunk The Stealer, Mummers, Dancin' to Calliope, The Kiss, The Man in The Water.*

Awards: NEA, Shubert Fellowship, five Ford Foundation productions, PEN Guest Artist grant, Carnegie Fund grant.

Contact: Jack Gilhooley, 639 West End Ave., New York, NY 10025

Philip Kan Gotanda

Plays: *A Song for a Nisei Fisherman, The Dream of Kitamura, The Wash, Yankee Dawg You Die, Fish Head Soup.*

Awards: NEA, Rockefeller, McKnight, Joseph Kesselring.

Contact: Helen Merrill, 361 W. 17th St., New York, NY 10011

Amlin Gray

Plays: *Zones of the Spirit, Kingdom Come, The Fan-*

tod, How I Got That Story, Namesake, and translations from Spanish and German.

Awards: Obie, NEA, Rockefeller, Guggenheim.

Contact: Lois Berman, 240 W. 44th St., New York, NY 10036

John Guare

Plays: *Landscape of the Body, Bosoms and Neglect, The House of Blue Leaves, Gardenia, Two Gentlemen of Verona, A Day for Surprises, Something I'll Tell You Tuesday, Loveliest Afternoon of the Year, Lydie Breeze, Rich and Famous, Marco Polo Sings a Solo, In Fireworks Lie Secret Codes, Home Fires, Kissing Sweet, Muzeeka, To Wally Pantoni I Leave a Credenza.* Screenplays: *Atlantic City, Taking Off.*

Awards: Obie, Outer Critics Circle Award, N.Y. Critics Circle Award, L.A. Drama Critics Circle Award, N.Y. Drama Critics Prize, two Tony Awards, two Rockefeller Grants.

Contact: Andrew Boose, 1 Dag Hammerskjold Plaza, New York, NY 10017

Oliver Hailey

Plays: *Hey You Light Man, Father's Day, Who's Happy Now* (PBS Theatre in America series), *Red Rover, Red Rover, I Won't Dance,* and *24 Hours* A.M. & P.M. and *The Bar Off Melrose.*

Awards: Drama Desk Award.

Contact: Shirley Bernstein, Paramuse Artists Associates, 1414 Ave. of the Americas, New York, NY 10019

Laura Harrington

Plays: *Night Luster, Free Fall, 'Round Midnight, Cheat, Angel Face, Women and Shoes, The Wrong Man.*

Screenplays: *Sonia, Secrets, The Original Colored House of David, The Listener, Ah!*
Opera/Music Theatre: *Lucy's Lapses, Countdown, Martin Guerre.*
Awards: New England Emmy, Quebec Cinemateque, Joseph Kesselring, Canadian Theatre Grant, FDG/CBS finalist.
Contact: Mary Harden, Bret Adams, Ltd., 448 W. 44th St., New York, NY 10036

Willy Holtzman

Plays: *Bovver Boys, San Antonio Sunset, Inside/Out, Opening Day.*
Awards: Semi-finalist CBS/FDG New Plays Contest.
Contact: Mary Harden, Bret Adams, Ltd., 448 W. 44th St., New York, NY 10036

William Inge

Plays: *Come Back Little Sheba, Picnic, Bus Stop, The Dark at the Top of the Stairs, A Loss of Roses, Natural Affection, Where's Daddy.*
Awards: Pulitzer Prize, Drama Critics Circle Award, Outer Circle Award, George Jean Nathan Award, Theatre Time Award.
Contact: Samuel French, 25 W. 45th St., New York, NY 10036

David Ives

Plays: *The Land of Cockaigne, Lives and Deaths of the Great Harry Houdini, Ancient History, Money in the Bank, Words, Words, Words, Sure Thing, A Singular Kinda Guy, Mere Mortals.*
Contact: c/o New Dramatists, 424 W. 44th St., New York, NY 10036

Jeffrey M. Jones

Plays: *Tomorrowland, Der Inka Von Peru, 70 Scenes of Halloween, The Confessions of a Dope Fiend, Nightcoil.*

Contact: c/o New Dramatists, 424 W. 44th St., New York, NY 10036

Lee Kalcheim

Plays: *Match-Play & A Party for Divorce, An Audible Sigh, Prague Spring, Win With Wheeler, Breakfast with Les and Bess, Friends, Big Bill, I'd Rather Be in Philadelphia, Moving.*

Awards: Emmy Award (for *All in the Family*), Christopher Medal and Writers Guild Award (ABC Afterschool Special).

Contact: Bret Adams, Ltd. 448 W. 44th St., New York, NY 10036

Jeffrey Kindley

Plays: *Among Adults, The Counterpart Cure, Saint Hugo of Central Park, Is There Life After High School?*

Awards: E.P. Conkle Playwrights Workshop Grant.

Contact: Gilbert Parker, William Morris Agency, Inc., 1350 Ave. of the Americas, New York, NY 10019

Sherry Kramer

Plays: *Partial Objects, About Spontaneous Combustion, The Release of a Live Performance, Wall of Water, Nano and Nicki in Boca Raton.*

Awards: NEA, N.Y. Foundation for the Arts Fellowship.

Contact: Sherry Kramer, 2525 Sheridan, Springfield, MO 65804

Harding Lemay

Plays: *Little Birds Fly, From a Dark Land, The Joslyn Circle, Death of Eagles, Look at Any Man.*

Contact: c/o New Dramatists, 424 W. 44th St., New York, NY 10036

Romulus Linney

Plays: *Childe Byron, Tennessee, Laughingstock, Democracy and Esther, Holy Ghosts, Heathen Valley, April Snow, The Captivity of Pixie Shedman, El Hermano, Gardens of Eden, Old Man Joseph and His Family, The Sorrows of Frederick.*
Fiction: *Jesus Tales, Heathen Valley.*
Awards: Obie, Award in Literature from the American Academy and Institute of Arts and Letters, NEA, Guggenheim, Rockefeller, N.Y. Foundation for the Arts.
Contact: Gilbert Parker, William Morris Agency, 1350 Ave. of the Americas, New York, NY. 10019

Robert N. Lord

Plays: *China Wars, The Traveling Squirrel, Bert and Maisy, Country Cops.*
Awards: Burns Fellow, Univ. of Otage, New Zealand; Dramalogue Award Best Writing, CAPS Grant.
Contact: Gil Parker, William Morris, 1350 Ave. of the Americas, New York, NY 10019

Matthew Maguire

Plays: *The Memory Theatre of Giulio Camillo, Propaganda, Visions of Don Juan, Fun City, The American Mysteries, Untitled (The Dark Ages Flat out).* Co-artistic director of Creation Production Company.
Contact: Creation Production Company, 127 Greene St., New York, NY 10012

Dennis McIntyre

Plays: *Modigliani, Split Second, National Anthems, Established Price.*

Awards: NEA, Playbill Award, Rockefeller Grant for Production, MCA Fellowship in Playwriting, Tufts University Commission for Playwriting.
Contact: Howard Rosenstone, 3 E. 48th St., New York, NY 10017

Grace McKeaney

Plays: *Last Looks, Chicks, Fits and Starts, How It Hangs, Deadfall, Blue Moon.*
Awards: NEA, Le Compte de Nouy, Artistic Associate, Center Stage, Baltimore, O'Neill Theatre Conference Playwright, Sundance Institute.
Contact: Pat Quinn, ICM, 8899 Beverly Blvd., Beverly Hills, CA 90048, or, Mary Meagher, Gersh Agency, 130 W. 42nd St., New York, NY 10036

Ellen McLaughlin

Plays: *Little Kindnesses, Stranger in the Mountain, Days and Nights Within, A Narrow Bed.*
Awards: Susan Smith Blackburn Prize, Winner Actors Theatre of Louisville Great American Play Contest, currently Playwright in Residence at the Juilliard School.
Contact: Joyce Ketay, 334 W. 89th St., 4F, New York, NY 10024

John Nassivera

Plays: *The Penultimate Problem of Sherlock Holmes, Phallacies, Making a Killing.*
Awards: NEA Playwriting Fellowship.
Contact: Bill Craver, Writers and Artists Agency, 70 W. 36th St., #501, New York, NY 10018

Eric Overmyer
Plays: *Native Speech, On the Verge, In a Pig's Valise, In Perpetuity Throughout the Universe.*
Awards: Le Comte de Nouy, McKnight, N.Y. Foundation for the Arts.
Contact: George Lane, William Morris Agency, 1350 Ave. of the Americas, New York, NY 10019

Oyamo (Charles F. Gordon)
Plays: *Resurrection of Lady Lester, A Hopeful Interview with Satan.*
Awards: NEA, Rockefeller, Guggenheim, three O'Neill Playwrights Conference.
Contact: Anna Marie McKay, Inc., 400 W. 43rd St., #3A, New York, NY 10036

John Pielmeier
Plays: *Agnes of God, Sleight of Hand, Haunted Lives, Boys of Winter, Courage.*
Screenplays: *Choices of the Heart.*
Awards: ATL Great American Play Contest for *Agnes of God*, Shubert Fellow, Christopher Award.
Contact: Jeanine Edmunds, 230 W. 55th St., Suite 29D, New York, NY 10019

Allan Rieser
Plays produced: *Lady on a Leash, The Crystal Cage, The Merry Wives of Scarsdale, The Brownstone Urge* (with Gladys Foster), *Time Again* (musical, with Don Price and James Campodonica), *The Elysian Fields.*
Plays published: *A Jar of Marmalade, Boy Meets Family, You're Fired.*
Contact: Allan Rieser, 7 W. 96th St., #2C, New York, NY 10025

BIOGRAPHIES OF PLAYWRIGHTS

Sheldon Rosen
Plays: *Souvenirs, Ned & Jack, The Box, Frugal Repast, Uncle Marjoe, Stag King.*
Awards: Canadian Author's Assoc. Award for Drama, three Canada Council grants, three Ontario Arts Council grants.
Contact: Joyce Ketay, 334 W. 89th St., 4F, New York, NY 10024

Robert Schenkkan
Plays: *Final Passages, The Survivalist, Tall Tales, Lunchbreak, Intermission, Tachi Nakei.*
Awards: CAPS, "Best of the Fringe Award" Edinburgh Festival.
Memberships: New Dramatists, Ensemble Studio Theatre (N.Y./L.A.)
Contact: Helen Merrill Agency, 361 W. 17th St., New York, NY 10011

June Septant (Sydney Chandler)
Plays: *Nibs, Love and Loathing in Postwar Paris, The Summer's Over and We Have Not Been Saved.*
Contact: Sydney Chandler, 728 Amsterdam Ave., #3N, New York, NY 10025

John Patrick Shanley
Plays: *Danny and the Deep Blue Sea, Savage in Limbo, the dreamer examines his pillow, Welcome to the Moon, Rockaway, Gorilla, Saturday Night at the War.*
Screenplays: *Moonstruck, Five Corners.*
Awards: NEA, Rinehart Foundation.
Contact: Jeanine Edmunds, 230 W. 55th St., Suite 290, New York, NY 10019

William J. Sibley
Plays: *Governor's Mansion, If You Loved Me, Lock the Doors, Mr. & Mrs. Coffee, Mortally Fine, Two Men, Two Women.*
Screenplay: Adaptation of D. H. Lawrence's *St. Mawr.*
Other: Contributing Editor of *Flying Colors* and *Interview* magazines, Guest Playwright at the 1984 STAGES Texas Playwright's Festival, Houston; Playwright in Residence, Blue Mountain Center, N.Y.
Awards: Winner Southwest Regional Playwright's Competition.
Contact: Susan Breitner, 1650 Broadway, #501, New York, NY 10019

Steven Somkin
Plays: *The Grandchild Lust of Madeleine Lefferts, John Anderson, The American Oasis, Andahazy.*
Contact: Timothy J. DeBaets, Stults & Marshall, 1370 Ave. of the Americas, New York, NY 10019

Victor Steinbach
Plays: *The Bathers, My Life in Art, The Possessed.*
Awards: Playbill Award for *The Bathers,* N.Y. Foundation for the Arts, Helen Jean Arthur Foundation Grant.
Contact: Helen Merrill Agency, 361 W. 17th St., New York, NY 10011

Jeffrey Sweet
Plays: *The Value of Names, Porch, Ties, American Enterprise.*
Awards: NEA, N.Y. Foundation for the Arts, Outer Critics Circle
Award: Heideman Award.

Contact: Susan Schulman, 454 W. 44th St., New York, NY 10036

Megan Terry
Plays: Author of more than fifty plays and musicals, among them *Viet Rock, Approaching Simone, Calm Down Mother, Hothouse, Retro, Sleazing Toward Athens.*
Awards: Guggenheim, Rockefeller, NEA.
Currently Playwright-in-residence and Literary Manager of The Omaha Magic Theatre.
Contact: Elisabeth Marton, 96 5th Ave., New York, NY 10011, or c/o The Omaha Magic Theatre, 1417 Farnam St., Omaha, NE 68102

Daniel Therriault
Plays: *Battery, The White Death, Floor Above the Roof.*
Awards: Drama-Logue Awards, "Ten Best" L.A. Times, Arthur Foundation and Hawaiian Humanities grants (for *The White Death*), winner Chicago Play Expo (for *Floor Above the Roof*).
Contact: Broadway Play Publishing, 357 W. 20th St., New York, NY 10011

Terri Wagener
Plays: *Renascence, The War Brides, The Man Who Could See Through Time, Tattler, Semi Precious Things, Damn Everything But the Circus.*
Awards: NEA, finalist twice for the Susan Smith Blackburn Award.
Contact: c/o Arthur Klein, Frankfort, Garbus, Klein & Selz, 485 Madison Ave., New York, NY 10022

Mac Wellman
Plays: *Starlustre, Harm's Way, The Self-Begotten, The*

Professional Frenchman, The Bad Infinity, Energumen, Cleveland, Nain Rouge, "1951", Dracula.
Awards: NYFFTA Fellow, Prix D'Italia runner-up for the Netherlands, CBS/FDG finalist.
Contact: Helen Merrill Agency, 361 W. 17th St., New York, NY 10011

August Wilson
Plays: *Ma Rainey's Black Bottom, Fences, Joe Turner's Come and Gone, The Piano Lesson.*
Awards: Tony, Pulitzer, Drama Desk Award, New York Drama Critics Award, Assoc. Playwright, Playwright's Center, Minneapolis, O'Neill Center Playwright 1982, 83, 84.
Contact: c/o New Dramatists, 424 W 44th St., New York, NY 10036

Lanford Wilson
Plays: *The Hot L Baltimore, Lemon Sky, Angels Fall, Serenading Louie, The Mound Builders, Balm in Gilead, The Rimers of Eldritch, Fifth of July, Talley's Folly, Talley and Son, Burn This.*
Awards: Pulitzer Prize New York Drama Critics Circle Award, Outer Critics Circle Award, Obie, Brandeis University Creative Arts Award in Theatre, Institute of Arts and Letters Award, Drama-Logue Award, Vernon Rice Award.
Contact: Bridget Aschenberg, ICM, 40 W. 57th St., New York, NY 10019

Dick D. Zigun
Plays: *Lucky Lindy, His Master's Voice, Red Letter Days, The Adventures of Alice E. Neuman.*
Awards: NEA, NYSCA, N.Y. Foundation for the

Arts, N.Y.C. Dept. of Cultural Affairs, John Golden
Foundation.
Zigun is artistic director of Coney Island, USA, New
York City.
Contact: Coney Island, USA, Inc, Boardwalk @ W.
12th St., Coney Island, NY 11224

There's an epidemic with 27 million victims. And no visible symptoms.

It's an epidemic of people who can't read.

Believe it or not, 27 million Americans are functionally illiterate, about one adult in five.

The solution to this problem is you... when you join the fight against illiteracy. So call the Coalition for Literacy at toll-free **1-800-228-8813** and volunteer.

Volunteer Against Illiteracy. The only degree you need is a degree of caring.